Dominoes

RULES OF THE GAME

Backgammon
Darts
Dominoes
Go

RULES OF THE GAME

Dominoes

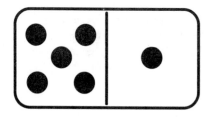

Gary Grady
Suzanne Goldberg

GAMESCAPE PUBLICATIONS
SAN FRANCISCO

First Gamescape Edition 1995

Published by Gamescape Publications
333 Divisadero Street
San Francisco, CA 94117

Printed in the United States of America

ISBN 1-887594-01-9

Contents

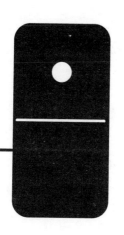

Preface

Dominoes is one in a series of books that make up the **Rules of the Game** library of popular pastimes. As with all books within this series, *Dominoes* is designed to introduce the beginning player to the game—in this case the large family of domino games—in a clear and simple manner. This book covers the basic rules and strategies of dominoes and introduces all the major games and their variations. A complete glossary defines the common terms associated with the game and their correct usage.

It is hoped that more experienced players will find much that is new to them in this book as well. The games included cover a broad cross section of skill levels and complexity. We have presented some simple games that both children and adults can enjoy together, and some challenging games for the more sophisticated players.

As you read the book you will come across words printed in **bold** type. These are some of the terms that appear in the glossary. If you are unclear about the definition or usage of a term, please refer to the glossary.

You may find that some of your favorite games are not listed in the index, but in all likelihood they are here under another name. Domino games tend to take on local names and variations, so read the game descriptions and find your old favorites and perhaps some entertaining new versions as well.

Domino games have been passed on from generation to generation and from friend to friend for hundreds of years. There has not been a governing body which has appropriated the authority to dictate the "official rules." Thus games will sometimes share names but have slight variations. Conversely, they may share rules but be known by different names in different regions—or even within different families.

For instance, Muggins and All Fives and Five-Up are all point games in which players score when the end points total a multiple of five. In some places these names may have become interchangeable. Yet in most places (and in this book) Five-Up is distinctly different, while Muggins and All-Fives are more similar.

In some cases the only difference might be in the number of tiles drawn to begin a game, how the setter is determined or whether or not doubles may be used as spinners. If you are new to dominoes, you may not understand the meaning of these terms. However, these are simple concepts which are explained in the early chapters. Once you understand them you can play virtually any domino game.

In *Dominoes* we have set down the rules for each game as we have determined they are most frequently played. We also mention alternative names and variations. We hope this will assist you as you learn new games or modify the rules to best conform to your own group's preferences.

Dominoes is one of the world's great games. It is played in every corner of the world, and we hope this book will bring you worlds of fun.

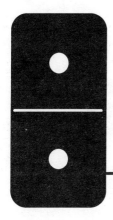

1
The Game

Dominoes refers to a family of games played with a set of tiles whose faces are marked with dots, called **pips**, that determine their value. The tiles are also referred to as dominoes and come in three standard sets.

The double-6 set consists of twenty-eight tiles and is so-called because the highest numbered tile incorporates a pair of six pips. The other two sets are also referred to by the number of pip pairs on the highest tile. They are the double-9 set, which contains fifty-five pieces, and the double-12 set which contains ninety-one pieces.

The double-6 set is the most common set of dominoes and the first part of this book will cover the games that are played with this set. We will consider the double-9 and the double-12 sets in a later chapter. Most of the games that are played with the double-6 set can also be played with the larger sets to allow more players or longer games.

You can create smaller sets of various sizes from larger sets. From a double-12 set, for example, you can create a double-6 or a double-9 set as well as any other lesser size such as a double-7 or

Figure 1-1. Chinese dice.

double-10. In later chapters we will examine some cases when you might choose to create these nonstandard sets.

In the next chapter we will take a closer look at the physical structure of the domino. This will be followed by chapters covering the rules and strategies for a large variety of domino games.

The origin of domino games has not been recorded. Like most popular games that were played by the common folk, they were not considered important enough for the historians to preserve. One aspect seems clear, however. Dominoes have a direct relationship to dice and most likely evolved from them. Dice are small cubes the six sides of which are marked by dots, also called pips, from one to six. Dice have been found in human settlements much older than recorded history. Dice have been used for lots and divination in most civilizations throughout the world. Figures 1-1 and 1-2 show dice from Chinese and Etruscan cultures and many anthropologists trace this common form to the Indus valley from which they were carried both east and west. But whether dice have a common origin or were developed independently it is clear that dominoes are the children of dice.

If we look at the surface of a pair of dice it is clear that the

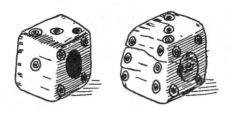

Figure 1-2. Etruscan dice, circa 900 B.C.

various combinations of those pairs are represented by the various dominoes. A pair of 6s would be represented by the 6-6, a roll of 5-4 would be equivalent to the 5-4 domino.

Figure 1-3 shows a complete set of Chinese dominoes. The top row shows the twenty-one dominoes that correspond to the twenty-one possible dice combinations. The lower row contains duplicates of some of the dominoes in the top row. The resulting complete set comprises a total of thirty-two dominoes. Games are still played throughout the Orient with the Chinese set. In recent years, Pai Gow, a Chinese and Korean game played with this set, has become a popular gambling game in the West

Figure 1-4 shows a set of European dominoes which contains twenty-eight tiles. Like the Chinese set described above, this set also includes dominoes corresponding to the twenty-one possible dice combinations. In this set, however, the extra dominoes come from the inclusion of a blank added to the series of pips. European dominoes have become the standard configuration now used worldwide.

As with dice, there is no direct evidence of where dominoes were first invented but indirect evidence would point to China.

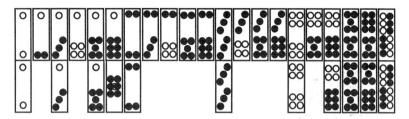

Figure 1-3. A complete set of Chinese dominoes.

The first record we have of dominoes in Europe is around the 14th century, but written records in China predate this appearance by hundreds of years. By the 14th century there was a well developed system of trade between the merchants of Italy and China and we can easily imagine the men of the caravans amusing themselves around the camp fire with this new game that they were taking home.

The durable tiles have always made dominoes an ideal game for travelers. Sailors have planted the game in every port and have made it an international pastime. The popularity of the game is also due to its easy-to-learn rules and the great enjoyment it offers.

Today dominoes is a popular family game and can be played by both children and adults alike. So take out your set of bones, gather your family and friends around, open this book to one of the many games it contains and have some fun!.

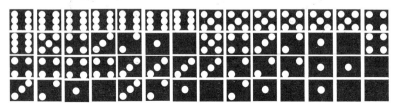

Figure 1-4. A complete set of European dominoes.

2
Dem Bones

The term dominoes describes a set of tiles that are used for a large variety of games. As the term "cards" describes any of the games that can be played with a standard 52-card deck of playing cards, so dominoes describes a family of games that can be played with a deck of domino tiles. The individual tiles are called by a variety of names: bones, stones, rocks and bricks just to name a few.

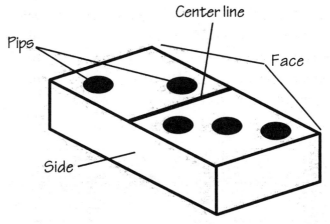

Fig. 2-1. The basic configuration of a domino.

Figure 2-1 shows the basic layout of a European domino. Dominoes come in an assortment of sizes, see Figure 2-4, and are constructed from a large variety of materials, but all will conform to this basic structure. The domino in Figure 2-1 is shown face up. The face of the domino contains the information and no two faces are alike. The back of the domino is blank or uniform in design. Domino backs should be indistinguishable from each other.

The face of the domino is divided into two equal parts by the center line. Each half of the domino is counted separately. Each spot, called a pip, is counted as one unit. Thus, ▪ one pip represents 1, two pips ▪ represent 2, and so on up to six pips which is the maximum for the double-6 set. The domino in Figure 2-1 shows two pips on the upper half of the tile and three pips on the lower portion of the tile and would be referred to as a 2-3 or a 3-2.

Double-Six

We will look first at the double-6 set. This refers to the fact that the highest number of pips is six on both halves of the domino. Figure 2-3 shows a complete set of double-6 dominoes. There are twenty-eight dominoes in the set with seven classified as doubles and twenty-one as singles. Figure 2-2 shows the seven doubles of the double-6 set. These doubles hold a special place in most games and will be covered in upcoming chapters.

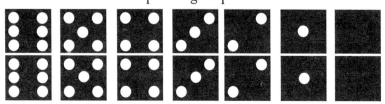

Fig. 2-2. The seven doubles.

There are twenty-one **singles**—dominoes whose two halves have different pip counts. Figure 2-3 shows the domino faces of a complete set. Like playing cards, dominoes can be classified into **suits**. In dominoes there are seven suits, one for each pip count (1-6) plus the blank. There are seven tiles in each suit, again 1-6 plus the blank. The single tiles will appear in two suits, one for each of the two pip counts found on the face. If we look at the bottom row in Figure 2-3 we can see the complete 6 suit that is made up of the 6-6, 6-5, 6-4, 6-3, 6-2, 6-1 and 6-blank. The complete 5 suit will consist of the 5-6, 5-5, 5-4, 5-3, 5-2, 5-1 and the 5-blank. As we can see, the 6-5 and 5-6 are the same tile and does service in both the 5 and 6 suits. We can build these seven-tile suits for each number and blank. When we make the notation 6-5 we refer to 6 suit with number 5, whereas 5-6 would refer to the 5 suit with the number 6. This is the same tile do-ing double work.

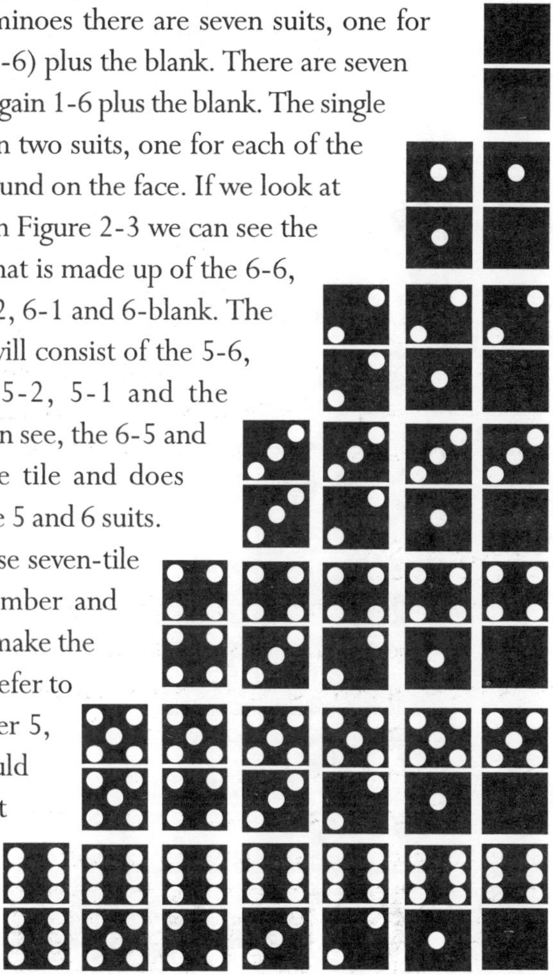

Fig. 2-3. The 28 tiles that make up a double-6 set of domino bones.

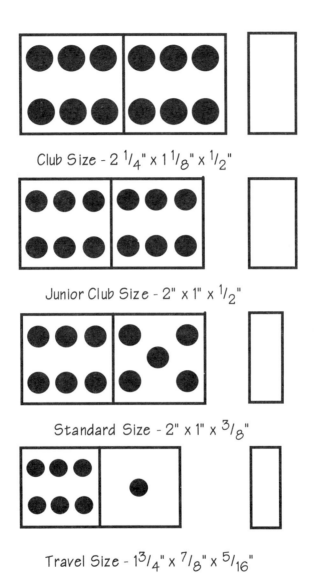

Club Size - 2 $^1/_4$" x 1 $^1/_8$" x $^1/_2$"

Junior Club Size - 2" x 1" x $^1/_2$"

Standard Size - 2" x 1" x $^3/_8$"

Travel Size - 1$^3/_4$" x $^7/_8$" x $^5/_{16}$"

Fig. 2-4. Standard domino sizes and thicknesses.

Dominoes come in a variety of sizes and are made of an even larger variety of materials. Figure 2-4 shows the standard sizes that are commonly available. The club size is the most comfortable to play with unless you are in the habit of holding your tiles in your hand, then a smaller size might be your choice. Most of us learned to play on the small black, wooden, dragon-back tiles given to us as children and these dragon dominoes are entirely sufficient. For the traveler, in addition to small dominoes, there are domino playing cards, regular-size playing cards with a set of dominoes printed upon their faces.

Dominoes have been made from every conceivable material—wood, ivory, stone, brass, aluminum, jade, and now plastic. From a practical point you should make sure that the material does not have recognizable individual patterns on the backs of the dominoes. This would be like playing with a marked deck. Some hard woods have very beautiful and distinctive grain patterns. It is these patterns that make the woods a joy to behold, but you would soon be able to recognize individual tiles in a domino set made from them.

A manufacturer once showed me a set of dominoes that he was making from a beautiful New Zealand hard wood—the pips and center line were inlaid ebony; they were a quality item. Within ten minutes I could pick out all of the doubles when the set was laid face down, the grain was so distinctive. Such individuality is simply not practical for a set you are going to use on a regular basis. So make sure that the set you buy does not exhibit this problematic characteristic.

Double-Nine

The double-9 set in which the highest tile is 9-9, consists of fifty-five pieces. The double-9 set consists of ten suits with ten

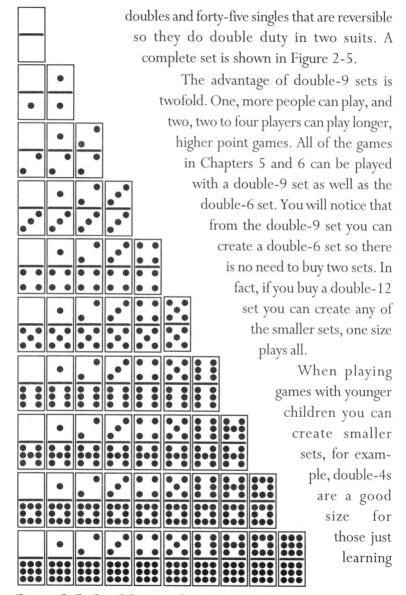

doubles and forty-five singles that are reversible so they do double duty in two suits. A complete set is shown in Figure 2-5.

The advantage of double-9 sets is twofold. One, more people can play, and two, two to four players can play longer, higher point games. All of the games in Chapters 5 and 6 can be played with a double-9 set as well as the double-6 set. You will notice that from the double-9 set you can create a double-6 set so there is no need to buy two sets. In fact, if you buy a double-12 set you can create any of the smaller sets, one size plays all.

When playing games with younger children you can create smaller sets, for example, double-4s are a good size for those just learning

Figure 2-5. The 55 tiles of the Double-9 set.

to count. The games will be short and the numbers manageable.

Double-Twelve

The double-12 set refers to the largest of the standard domino sets consisting of ninety-one pieces with the highest being the 12-12. The double-12 set contains 13 suits and again can be used for larger groups of players or longer games. The set will be explained in Chapter 7.

Scoreboard

A piece of equipment that is handy to have when playing most games of dominoes is a scoreboard. Figure 2-5 shows a basic scoreboard, more commonly called a **cribbage board** since it is an essential piece of equipment for that game, but it can be used to score many games including dominoes. The scoreboard, usually made of wood or plastic, consists of two series of sixty holes, divided into two rows of thirty, which are in turn divided into groups of five for ease of counting. Counting is done by each player moving

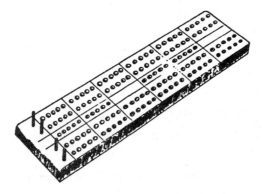

Figure 2-6. Scoreboard.

a peg one hole per point. Two pegs are supplied so that one is left as a reference point of the last score to which the new points are added from which they are counted.

Scoring is, of course, an important part of the game and it is up to each player to record his score accurately. If there is a mistake made in scoring it is up to the other players to point out that error before the next play takes place. If a mistake is made by your opponent that is in your favor you are under no obligation, other than the categorical imperative, to inform him of that mistake.

There are special boards designed for three players that come with continuous tracks of 120 points for cribbage games that can be used for dominoes if you play a lot of three-player games.

Paper and pencil can serve just as well in keeping track of points, but the scoreboard has the advantage that every player can see the score and his relationship to the other players. Many quality domino sets come in wooden cases that either have built-in scoreboards on the

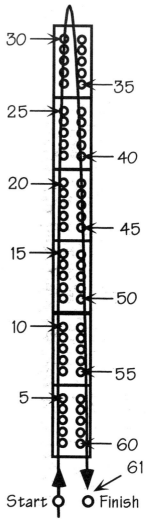

Figure 2-7

top of the case or contain a separate board. Once you get used to the peg scoreboard it will become an indispensable part of your gaming equipment.

3
General Rules

In this chapter we will look at the general rules of domino games. In the following chapters we will examine the rules for specific games and most of those will incorporate the general rules covered here. There are a number of terms used throughout this chapter and book that are necessary to understand the rules and strategy involved in mastering domino games. The first time an important word is used it will be highlighted and defined—all highlighted words can be found in the glossary. The rules that follow in this chapter pertain to the double-6 set of dominoes. The double-9 and double-12 sets are covered in a later chapter.

Deck: The deck refers to the complete set of dominoes. Unless stated otherwise, all games start with a complete deck. At the start of each game the deck is placed face down on the playing surface and **shuffled**. To shuffle the deck, one player will move the dominoes in a random manner until the deck is mixed and the value of the tiles is unknown to the players.

If you look at Figure 3-1 you will see a representation of a game table that we will use throughout this book. Dominoes is a very flexible game when it comes to the number of players but

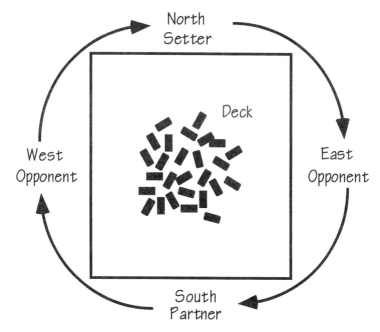

Figure 3-1. Seating arrangement and deck placement with direction of play.

two to four is common with the double-6 set. In many games it is common for four players to play as partners in two teams and some games are designed specifically for team play.

The first move is called the **set**, and the player who makes the first move is referred to as being **on set**. In many games the set is determined by the **draw**.

The term **on set** also refers to the person in the first position to "go out," that is, to play one's last domino. If the player on set is forced to go to the boneyard for more dominoes, he is then **off set**, and the next player with the fewest dominoes to play is now **on set**. This is of little significance except in serious team play. In most games you will have little control over this situation.

Draw: After the deck has been shuffled, each player draws, that is, takes from the deck, the number of dominoes that will make up the hand. In two-player games, each player picks seven tiles. In three- or four-player games, each player draws five dominoes. The remaining tiles become the **boneyard**. The draw can be done in seating order, starting with North followed by East, South and West. While some believe it contrary to etiquette for all players to draw from the deck simultaneously, others feel this is perfectly acceptable in casual play. Like many decisions in dominoes, this determination is one of player preference.

Once each player has drawn his allotted dominoes he places them on their sides so that the faces are visible to that player only (Figure 3-2). The backs of the tiles will be toward all other players. Some players prefer to hold the tiles in their hands. This is allowable and with some of the smaller size bones there is no problem, although with club size dominoes this may not be manageable. Player preference prevails.

Order of play: Once the draw has taken place and the players have examined their hands, the player with the highest double will play that double as the set **play** and that player becomes the **setter**. The highest double is, of course, the 6-6, but if it is not drawn the highest drawn double becomes the set play. It is

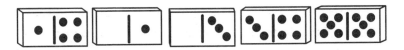

Figure 3-2. Drawn dominoes are placed in front of player on their sides so faces are visible only to the player who drew the hand.

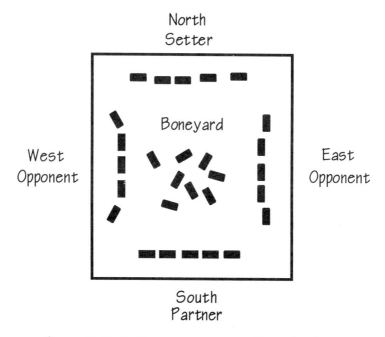

North
Setter

West
Opponent

Boneyard

East
Opponent

South
Partner

Figure 3-3. Table arrangement after the draw.

conceivable that the 1-1 or the double-blank could be the set play. If no double is drawn, all hands are discarded, the deck reshuffled and players redraw.

Once the setter is revealed play proceeds as shown in Figure 3-1. The setter is in the North position and play moves from his left.

In some games, however, the order of play is not determined by the draw. In these games the setter is determined by each player drawing one domino before the game begins, and the player who draws the tile with the highest total pip count becomes the setter. In the case of two dominoes with the same total, the higher domino is considered to be the one with the larger half. Thus a 6-3 is higher than a 5-4.

These dominoes are returned to the deck and the deck is then reshuffled. The setter takes the North position at the table. The next highest draw will sit to the setter's left and so on. If there is team play, the two highest draws and the two lowest draws will play as partners and will sit opposite each other.

Matching: The essence of domino play is matching tiles in your hand with the end of a line of dominoes that are in common play. The usual way of matching is by suits. In the last chapter we explained that the face of a domino is divided into two sections by a center line. Each of the resulting halves contains information in the form of dots, referred to as pips, from 0 to 6. Halves with the same pip count are of the same suit. In the standard double-6 set there are seven suits. The significance of suits will be covered in the next chapter. For our purposes it is only necessary to understand that like suits match.

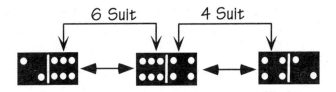

The seven doubles are playable only within their own suit. In other words, the double-5 is only able to match other 5s. Doubles are normally played across the line, and in some point games can be counted as twice their suit value when scoring, but for matching it is important to understand that doubles belong to only one suit while all single dominoes belong to two suits.

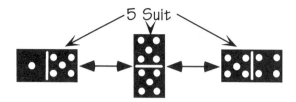

Not all matching is done by suits. Some matching requires a specific pip total of the two tiles. Matador and Russian Cross require end matches total seven, for example. When this situation arises it will be explained in the rules section for that specific game.

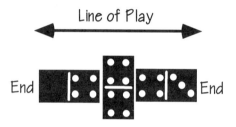

Figure 3-4. Line of play.

Line of play: This refers to the arrangement of the dominoes once play begins. The double is placed on the table perpendicular to the setter. In the example in Figure 3-4, the double-4 was set followed by East playing the 4-3 and South playing the 4-blank. It can be said that the doubles are played *across* the line of play whereas the singles are said to play *along* the line of play. If the 3-3 were to be played by West it would be placed next to the 3-end of the 4-3 across the line of play. If a line gets too long physically for the playing space, you can change the direction of the line of play by placing the next single at right angles to the old line of play (see Figure 3-5).

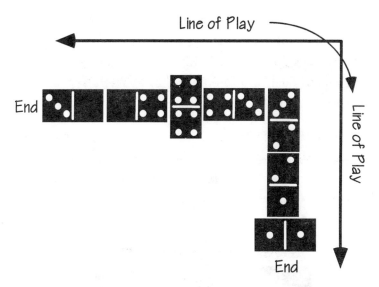

Figure 3-5. Turning the line of play.

Ends: In many games the ends of the line of play are important in scoring as well as matching. The pip count of the end sections are added and points scored depending on the total. In a number of games, points are scored if the total pip count is any multiple of five. In Figure 3-4 the end pip count is 3—the total of the three of the 4-3 and no points for the blank from the 4-blank single. If we add up the pips on the ends of the line shown in Figure 3-5 we will get a total of 5—three pips from the 3-blank and two from the 1-1. If a double is played across the line of play, the total pip value of both halves of the domino is counted.

Spinner: When a double is played across the line of play there is the possibility of playing off the ends as well as the sides. When rules allow this, that double is referred to as a **spinner**. Not all games allow doubles to be used as spinners. It is common to allow the first double played to be turned into a spinner, and a few games allow all doubles to become spinners, but you should consult the rules for each game. Many players modify the rules to suit their individual or group desire for spinners and they are often allowed under the optional rules.

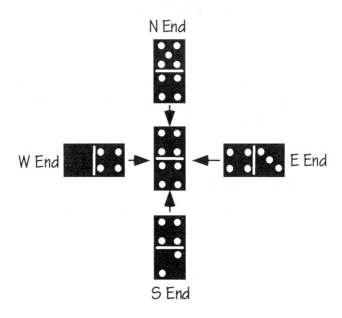

Figure 3-6. Spinner play.

Point count: All domino games are resolved by point counts. Point games are scored during the play of the dominoes as well as at the end of each hand. Block games are scored only after all play has ceased, either because one player has "dominoed" or the game is blocked. Some of the common scoring situations are shown in the following examples.

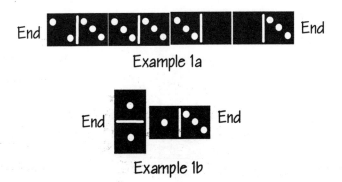

Example 1a

End ——— End

Example 1b

In Example 1 we see the two most common situations that will come up in every point game. To determine an end total we add the number of pips on each end. In Example 1a this would be $3+2=5$. In Example 1b the double-1 is valued at 2—end doubles are the sum of the pip values of both halves—and this is added to the 3 pips of the other end, $1+1+3=5$. There are games that allow scores to be made with the set tile. In point games that score off of fives, playing the double-5 as the set is worth 10 points.

End

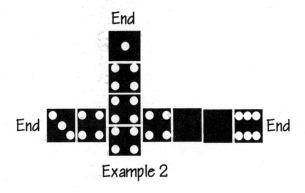

End   End

Example 2

In Example 2 the double-4 is a spinner with one end in play which now gives us three ends from which to score. An end total in this case would be $3+1+6=10$.

End

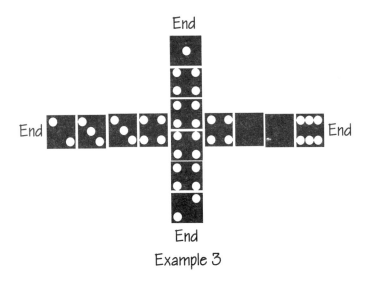

End   End

End

Example 3

In Example 3 both ends of the spinner are played giving four ends to count. This would give us $1+2+2+6=11$.

In Example 4 we have the situation where a double-6 is played on the end. When a double becomes an end the total pips are counted in the end count. In our example the double-6 would be counted as 12 points. End count in Example 4 would be $12+1+2+2=17$ points.

The more spinners in the line of play, the more complicated the structure and the end count. In Example 5 there are six ends that have to be included in an end count, $1+6+1+2+2+2=14$. Once a spinner is played off of, the newly created end will remain in play throughout the game. By playing a blank on any end, that end's points will be lost. For example, if a blank-3 is played off of the double-3 in Example 5 the end count would reduce to 8, $1+0+1+2+2+2$. It is important to think in terms of addition *and* subtraction when evaluating your hand. There will be times

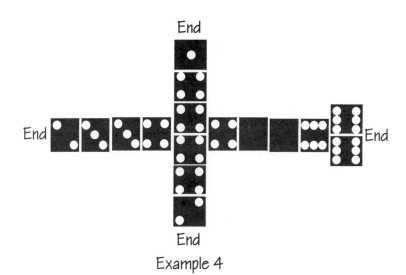

Example 4

when the boneyard has been exhausted and players are forced to pass. In this situation (and in certain games such as Seven Go) you will have the opportunity to play two tiles in a row, so think ahead. You must constantly adjust your tile play to the changing end count.

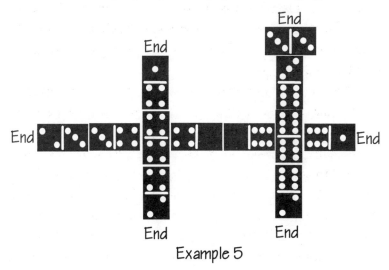

Example 5

Not all games are concerned with end point counts. The Block games presented in Chapter 5 do not involve end counts, but the mental dexterity that you develop in Point games will serve you well in all tile play.

Errors & Misplays

During a game there is the possibility of mistakes in play and procedures occurring. Most of these errors can be handled informally between the players with the guidelines below. If any error or indiscretion is noticed you should bring it to the attention of the perpetrator before making your move or allowing the next play to be made. In most cases if a misplay or error occurs during play it can be corrected at the time, but if play continues the play is let stand. If an error is made by your opponent that is to your benefit you are not required to inform him or demand correction. Errors can be grouped into four main categories:

Misplayed Dominoes

1. If a player plays a domino in conflict with the rules of the game any player may demand that the play be corrected. If there is a correct play for the the misplayed domino it must be made. If there is no correct play, the misplayed domino must be withdrawn and another domino played correctly. The misplayed domino is not placed back into the player's hand. Instead it is laid face up in front of the player. The player still controls this domino but is penalized for his error by having the domino exposed to his opponents for the remainder of the hand. This exposed domino must be played at the first opportunity.

2. If a domino has been misplayed but is not discovered until

after another domino has been played, the misplayed domino will remain in position and play will continue. Any score made by the misplayed domino will stand.

3. If a player plays out of turn and the next play has not been made the misplayed domino will be removed from the line, placed face up in front of the player and played at the first opportunity as described above.

4. If a player plays out of turn and the next play has taken place, play continues in the new order. All scores stand.

Exposed Dominoes

"Exposed domino" refers to any domino whose face is exposed to or seen by other players at inappropriate times. This exposure can be accidental or intentional.

1. If a player accidentally exposes a domino from his hand he must then turn that tile face up where it remains for all players to see. This domino must be played at the first opportunity.

2. If a domino is exposed while being drawn by a player, the player is forced to accept that domino and it will also be placed face up in front of her. As in the case of other exposed tiles, this domino must be played at the first opportunity.

3. If a domino in the boneyard is exposed in some manner not involved in a draw, it is shown to all the players, returned to the boneyard and the boneyard is reshuffled.

4. If a domino is intentionally exposed the player exposing the tile will be penalized by awarding his opponent(s) 5 points.

Overdraw

1. If a player takes more dominoes during the draw than he is entitled to, he must keep the extras that he has looked at. If he notices his error before turning the extras over, he may return them to the boneyard.

2. If a player overlooks a playable domino and draws from the boneyard he must keep the tiles drawn in error. It is difficult for other players to determine when a player has drawn from the boneyard in error and it is up to the honesty of each player to make her error known. The misdrawn tiles are treated like exposed dominoes and are placed face up in front of the player and must be played as soon as possible.

If another player points out the error before the perpetrator, she can not only require the exposure of the misdrawn dominoes, she may also request a penalty of 5 points.

3. If either of the last two dominoes are drawn from the boneyard, they should be returned and placed face up for all the players to see.

Underdraw

If a player draws fewer dominoes than the rules require, he must make up the shortage from the boneyard as soon as the error is discovered. If there are no dominoes remaining in the boneyard, the player can continue to play but he can not score points for going out.

You should now have an understanding and grasp of the basic rules of dominoes. In upcoming chapters we will describe individual games and their specific rules. The rules in this chapter will apply to most of the games and should be used as a guide unless otherwise stated.

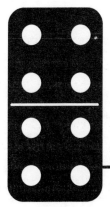

4

Basic Strategy

The basic strategy presented in this chapter will have applicability to most domino games. The games in the following chapters are divided into two families, point games and block games. Point games refer to games that are scored as the game progresses whereas block games are those which are scored only at the end of each hand. Both types of games are, of course, variations on the basic structure of dominoes, and most of the ideas covered in this chapter can be applied to both.

The double-6 set will be used in all of our examples, but most of these games can also be played with the double-9 and double-12 sets allowing you to increase the number of players to more than four. The double-9 set will also make for longer games with higher point totals. Basically the double-9 and double-12 sets increase your options in most games. It must be noted that sets of any size can be created from the larger sets; for example, a double-7 or a double-8 set can be built from a double-9 set.

Smaller sets can also be used as well as larger sets. Double-3 or double-4 sets are ideal for children's games. Dominoes can be a good learning tool for children; basic math skills and memory development are essential components of domino games. So keep in mind the various options open to you and the great flexibility offered by *dem bones*.

Suit Management: As we explained in previous chapters, the face of the domino is divided in two by a center line. The two faces created by the center line will contain the pips, or blank, that will govern the value of that particular tile. Each of the twenty-one single dominoes can be either one of two suits, and you the player determine the suit. Dominoes are not like playing cards with fixed suits—clubs, spades, hearts, and diamonds—that define the card's category and how it is played in the game. The domino in Figure 4-1 can have the suit value of either 5 or 4. The two views of the 5-4 tile in Figure 4-2 do not represent two different dominoes. This is merely a graphical demonstration of the fact that a single domino can fill either place within the diagram of a complete depiction of suits.

What is it that determines the suit? There is no hard and fast answer to this question. It is the total group of dominoes contained in your hand that will decide *your* choice of suit.

The concept of suit management refers to the decisions that players must make in evaluating and playing their hands. We will look at a number of basic tactics that you will use in building your overall strategy. These tactical concepts can be presented under the following headings: *suit determination and control, repeaters and kickers, playback and lead-back*.

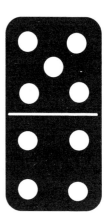

Figure 4-1

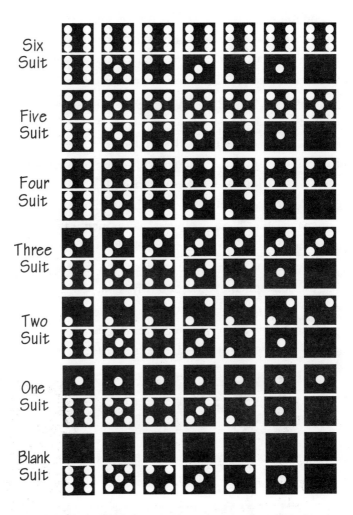

Six
Suit

Five
Suit

Four
Suit

Three
Suit

Two
Suit

One
Suit

Blank
Suit

Figure 4-2. The seven complete suits of a standard twenty-eight piece domino set. The twenty-one single dominoes do double duty and appear in two suits giving a total of forty-nine possible playing pieces.

The following discussion of strategy might be too advanced for beginning players. Remember that the following chapters include samples of numerous games. In these detailed examples we attempt to explain the reasoning and strategy involved in their play. As you become more familiar with various domino games you will want to refer back to these pages.

Suit Determination: Although there is some value in comparing the suits of dominoes with those of their pasteboard brother the playing card, the comparison is not an apt one. The four suits of the common deck of playing cards are predetermined and unchangeable. The suits found in dominoes offer some flexibility to the player. The player may pick either of the two numbers on the face of the twenty-one singles to be the suit or she may ignore the concept completely. So why is the concept important? There are two principal reasons.

Hand organization is the main reason one groups one's draw into suits. Let us look at this random seven-tile draw.

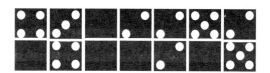

Figure 4-3. Reorganize your tiles by number. This will enable you to better analyze your hand.

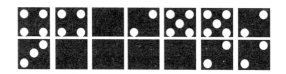

The hand shown in Figure 4-3 has several strong points. There are four tiles with blanks, the double-blank and three singles, as well as two other singles, the 4-3 and 5-2, that will play off two of the blank singles. The blanks will become our main suit. The two "5" tiles, blank-5 and 5-2, will play a special role discussed later.

To understand the value of declaring the blanks as a suit we must keep in mind two chief aims of individual hand play. These two primary objectives are: *get rid of your dominoes fast* and *stay out of the boneyard!* Every tile is a double-edged sword; it can score points for you or, if you are left holding the tile after an opponent has gone out, it can score points against you. By defining your main suit you can create a play strategy. The first consideration in building this strategy will depend on your order of play.

If the hand shown in Figure 4-3 is the setter's hand the blank suit is a strong set play. With four of the seven blank tiles you hold almost 60% of the suit. The double-blank as the set play would not give the opponents much of a chance to play off of it and there is a strong likelihood of sending them to the boneyard, including your partner in a four-hand game.

Of course your strength is also your weakness. In our example the player is absent in the six and one suits and might easily be sent to the boneyard herself. But even if you are not on set a strong suit will give you a chance to gain control of the line. It is a good exercise to play out your hand and see how many dominoes can be played. It is not possible to actually play this out in most real game situations but it gives you a good feel for your playback chances.

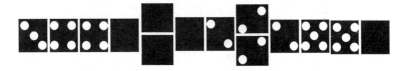

There are a number of considerations that you should take into account when evaluating a hand. The first is your position of play. If you are on set your choices are going to be mainly determined by the set rules of the game you are playing. If the rules require a double to be played your choice is limited to the doubles in your hand. If you can play any tile as set then your considerations are going to be determined by the type of game, point or block. In the five-point family of games, the 6-4, 4-1, double-5, and 5-blank will score as set plays. Of these four the 6-4 and 4-1 are the better plays because of the great value of the double-5 and 5-blank as **repeaters** and **kickers**.

Repeaters and Kickers: A key to a winning strategy is the ability to play off previous scoring end combinations. This is accomplished by playing **repeaters** and **kickers**, which consist of the blanks, the 5-suit, the 6-1, as well as those tiles that will play off their double and repeat the score, as when a 3-6 is played on the double-3. Let us look at the diagram below.

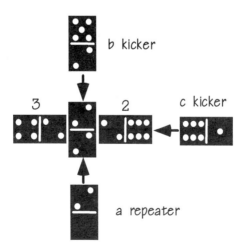

The sequence of play was the double-2 for set, followed by the 2-6 and then the 2-4 for an end total of 10 and a score. There are three possible ways to score on the next play if the double-2 is a spinner. The 2-blank at *a* is an example of a repeater—the end count does not change and the play of *a repeats* the score of 10 points. Play *b,* the 2-5, is a kicker and adds 5 points to the previous end total, in this case resulting in a score of 15 points. The third play, *c,* is the kicker 6-1, and its play would result in a scoring end count of 5.

When the set play is not a spinner but is a double the value of repeaters and kickers is diminished but they are still essential concepts of play. The simplest form is shown below. The double-4

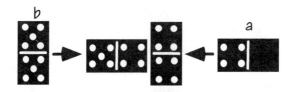

is played as set followed by the play of the 4-5 which scores no points since the end total is 13. If the next play is the 4-blank it will score with 5 points. While blank singles are often played as repeaters, this domino does not fill such a role in this case. If the double-5 play follows it will also score points but here it fulfills its role as a kicker. The line can be kicked again with the play of the blank-5 giving an end total of 15. The ends are now open to play

only by fives. There are no tiles that are available to repeat or kick the score with no spinners in play, but future plays should be made with these concepts in mind. As when playing card games, it is important for players to plan their moves and to keep track of the dominoes in their hand and in the line. In the above line three of the seven fives and fours have been played and these odds can be figured into future plays.

Leadback and playback: The concepts of leadback and playback involve sophisticated dominoes strategy and are most useful when playing as partners. They provide a framework for planning one's moves as well as describing the function of certain tiles. In other words, these terms refer to both the intentional, tactical play of the dominoes as well as simply describing how they function as the game progresses.

This is basically a two-step process where "leadback" refers to the first number and tile and "playback" refers to the play of the second tile. We have already explained that the twenty-one single dominoes can belong to either of two suits. The player makes the mental determination as to a tile's suit. The other number becomes the **suit number**. For example, if your hand includes the double-6, 6-4 and 6-3, you consider these as members of the 6-suit. Doubles have no leadback numbers. The "4" and the "3" in this example are suit numbers. They are also **leadback numbers**. Leadback tiles then become other single dominoes with either a 3 or a 4.

In our example, we set the double-6 (which is not a spinner) and our opponent played the 6-5. We followed with the 6-4. When the opponent plays the 4-3, he does not know that this is a leadback to the 3-6 in our hand. Of course, this may be his only

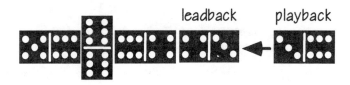

play, in which case even if he suspected that it might be a leadback he would still be forced to play it. When the 4-3 leadback is played it opens the way for our 3-6 playback.

As your dominoes strategical thinking becomes more sophisticated, you will begin to realize more possibilities. Imagine for a moment that you are the opponent in this scenario. You suspect that the other player may have a strong 6-suit. Why would you suspect this? Because the only 6-tile you hold is the 6-5. If you want to play away from this suspected 6-suit, you would optimally like to leave an end number of either 4 or 5 because these are no longer leadback numbers for the 6-suit. However, the 3-suit is your strongest suit. Your only plays on this layout are the 4-3 or the 5-3—either turns out to be a leadback to your opponent's 3-6.

The preceding discussion should suggest the intricacies of advanced domino strategy. However, no matter how well you might deduce your opponent's position, you are still bound by the tiles in your hand and the position of the layout. Remember, one of the beauties of dominoes is the fact that it can be played on many different levels, from the simplest to the most complex.

A general statement of domino strategy could be that the domino which gives you the greatest number of options is your best play. The only exception to this is when you know from previous plays the strengths and weaknesses of your opponent's

hand. For example, let us look at the layout shown above. In this situation player B goes to the boneyard. Thus we can assume that the player has no tiles of the 1 and 2 suits. Player B then draws a tile from the boneyard and plays it as shown in the diagram. Player A holds the two tiles as shown. One, the 4-3, will score points.

Player B

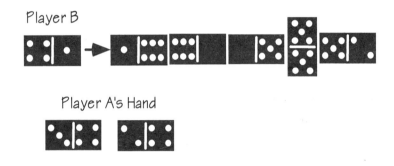

Player A's Hand

Should that be the play? Or should A play the 4-2 and send player B back to the boneyard? In most cases sending him to the boneyard is the best play as it is to your advantage to force more dominoes into your opponent's hand. However, you will have to evaluate the other variables such as the current score and how many tiles your opponent already holds.

Again, remember your primary objectives during play are to get rid of your dominoes as fast as possible and to stay out of the boneyard. Naturally, in point games it is also important to score points.

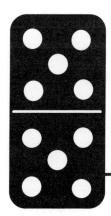

5
Block Games

The general characteristic of block games is that scoring does not take place during hand play but is only scored after play is complete. Block game strategy is, as the name implies, to block your opponent from playing his hand, to force him to the boneyard, and to go out as quickly as possible.

Block games are best played with four players in either teams or as cutthroat games. They are also easily adaptable to the larger size sets, double-9s and double-12s, and are thus best for larger group play. This is in no way meant to imply that they are not excellent games for two or three players as well. In addition, they are undoubtedly the best domino games for beginning younger players.

Most of the strategy and rules that you have encountered so far will apply to block games. Suit management is still central to good play but end scores are ignored. This lack of scoring during hand play makes the tiles more ecumenical and the only consideration is the efficiency of play. To go out first is the primary strategical consideration when it comes to block games.

Block

Players: Two, three and four players. Four players may play as a
   team. Suitable for children as young as five.

Draw & Set: For two players, each draws seven tiles. Three players,
   six tiles each; four players draw five tiles. Player with the highest
   double is on set. If no double, shuffle and redraw.

Object: To match ends according to suit; to be the first player to
   domino to win hand and score points remaining in the hand(s)
   of opponent(s).

Play:

   Block is the simplest and most basic of the domino games. As
with all block games in this chapter, no scoring is done during
play. Dominoes are played in one line; doubles are played across
the line but cannot be used as spinners. Each play must match the
suit of the set play double and the suits of the subsequent ends. A
player must make a match on his turn. If a player has no matching
suit in his hand he must go to the boneyard and draw until he
makes a match. As in all domino games, the last two dominoes
must be left in the boneyard in a two-player game; one in a three-
or four-player game. If a player cannot make a match and no
dominoes are left to be drawn from the boneyard, the player must
pass. Game continues until one player goes out or until the game
is **blocked** and no one has a play.

   For two players game is 61 points; three and four players,
121 points. A point is scored by the winner for each pip remaining
in an opponent's hand.

Sample   Game:

   The following two-player game is between Myra and Dave.

Dave places all of the dominoes face down on the table and shuffles them. Each selects seven tiles from the deck and these become their hands. The remaining tiles become the boneyard and are pushed to the side.

Myra's Draw:

Myra has drawn a very good hand. The double-6 guarantees that Myra will play set, and this is a big advantage in Block. Adding to her good fortune is a strong 6-suit. With four out of the seven tiles of that suit she may be able to put some pressure on Dave.

Dave's Draw:

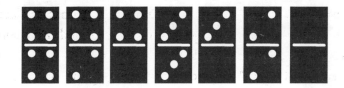

Dave's hand does not offer a high degree of versatility. You can see the advantage of set play here. If Dave were able to play his double-4 as set he would be in good shape, but if he must respond to set play he has no play against 1, 5 or 6. Myra has at least one play in all suits.

Myra plays the double-6 and sends Dave to the boneyard on his first turn. Dave has some luck in drawing a 6-3 on his first draw and plays it against the 6-6. Play unfolds as shown below.

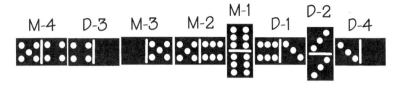

The play is straightforward after Myra's set play of the 6-6. Dave plays his 6-3; Myra her 6-5. The next several plays unfold as shown above. Since no scoring is made during this part of the game one of the main considerations is to get rid of the highest pip counts that you can play since you will be penalized for any dominoes you still hold at the end of the hand. However, the most important consideration when you have a choice is to play a domino that will leave an end suit from which you can play and which might force your opponent to the boneyard.

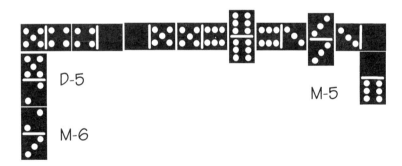

When Myra plays her blank-6 she sends Dave to the boneyard again. His first draw is a blank-2 which he cannot play. He draws again and gets a playable 5-2. Myra is down to two tiles and can play off of either end. She knows that Dave does not have a 6 so she decides to play the 2-3. She knows that this is the fourth play of the 3-suit. She hopes to send Dave to the boneyard again. She does.

Dave draws a 4-1 and a 5-1 before he draws a playable 4-3 which he plays to the 3-end. Myra plays her 6-1 and calls out "domino" to show that she has played all her dominoes and has won the hand.

Scoring:

Myra now scores all the points in Dave's hand. Dave is left holding seven tiles, a painful loss. Here is how it is scored:

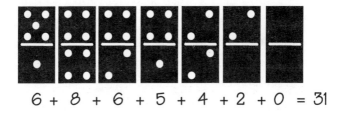

6 + 8 + 6 + 5 + 4 + 2 + 0 = 31

The total pip count of Dave's remaining dominoes is 31 points. This becomes Myra's score. A game is played to 61 points so Myra has 30 points to go.

When a game becomes blocked, that is, no player has "dominoed," no one has a play, and everyone has passed at least once, the hand is declared over. Each player totals his pips and the one with the lowest score is declared the winner. For example, let us say that a game between Myra and Dave ends in a block. Myra has two dominoes remaining for a pip total of 8 while Dave holds three dominoes for a total of 15 points. Myra is declared the winner because her score is lower. Her points are determined by subtracting her pip total from Dave's, 15-8=7, and this results in Myra's scoring 7 points.

These two methods of scoring will be used with most of the block games covered in this section. Remember, games are played to 61 points and will be made up of a number of hands. After one hand is completed the deck is shuffled and play follows the above format.

Variations:

There are several methods of determining which player is on set in both the first hand and in subsequent hands. Some people prefer to draw for set in which case any domino may be set.

You may choose to play that the loser of each hand (or the largest loser if more than two are playing) is on set for the next hand. Or you may choose to alternate as setter. In both cases you can play either that any domino may be set or that a double must be set, in which case the person on set may be forced to the boneyard if she has no double in her hand.

You may also choose to draw all the dominoes to begin the hand, eliminating the boneyard and subsequent drawing during the game. This is most common in a four-player game where each player draws seven dominoes. Of course, as you will continue to discover the more you play dominoes, there are variations on variations. In this case, some rules dictate that at least one domino always remain in the boneyard. Thus, when dealing all the tiles for Block, two players draw 13; three players, 9; and four, only 6.

In some regions the game we have described as Block is called **Draw** because players draw from the boneyard when they do not hold a playable domino. Block refers to the same game where the boneyard is not in use, either because all dominoes are dealt to begin the hand or simply where the boneyard is not used regardless of the number of tiles originally dealt. There is an additional variation known as **Pass** where the boneyard is in play but where players have the option of passing even when they hold a playable tile or when dominoes are available in the boneyard.

Cross

Players: Two, three and four players. Four players may play as a team; however, the Cross games are better played with four individual players.

Draw & Set: For two players, each draws seven tiles. Three players, six tiles each; four players draw five tiles. Player with the highest double is on set.

Object: To match ends by suits; to be first player to **domino** and score the points remaining in the opponents' hands.

Play:

Cross is a variation on Block with the basic rules applying. The main variation found in Cross is that the first double played must have a domino played from both the sides and ends before any other domino can be played. In the illustration below, the double-6 was set, and four dominoes of the 6-suit must be played off of the set domino before play can be made off the other suits. If a player does not have a match to the set double, he must go to

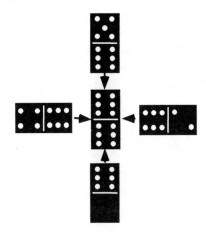

the boneyard and draw until he gets a match. If there are no playable dominoes left in the boneyard—two dominoes must remain—and a player still has no match, he must pass. Once the cross has been created play continues from any of the four ends.

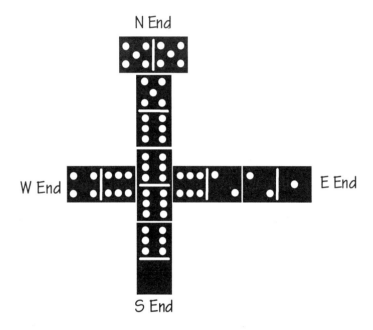

After the five-tile cross has been created, play continues off of the four ends and follows the rules as set forth in Block. The double-5 is played off the North End in the standard way, across the line of play. Doubles do not become spinners. The 2-1 is shown being played off the 6-2 at the East End, and again play is consistent with rules and examples given in the section on Block.

There are no significant strategical decisions to be made in Cross at the start of the game. The highest double must be played and all players must play off of it until the cross is completed. A player may not pass if she has a playable tile in her hand even if she has previously played off of the set double. Play continues until one player "dominoes" or all players are blocked.

Scoring:

Scoring is the same as described under the Block rules in cutthroat games. When four players are playing as teams the team that goes out first is awarded the total pip point count of the hands of both players of the losing team.

Variations:

Double Cross is a variant that increases the dimensions of the cross by requiring a double to be played on the four tiles that are played from the set double. All other rules for Cross and Block

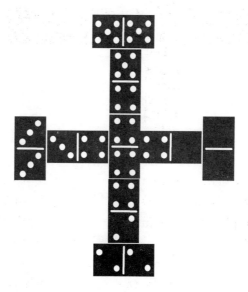

apply to this variation. The end doubles cannot be used as spinners and must be played from the side. Cross games are especially suited to play with the larger double-9 and double-12 sets.

Russian Cross

Players: Two, three and four players. Four players may play as teams.

Draw & Set: Two players draw seven dominoes from the shuffled deck. Three or four players draw five dominoes. The player with the highest double (double-blank excluded) sets. If no double, shuffle and draw again.

Object: To match ends that total the sum of seven. The first player to domino wins the hand and scores the pip points held by opponent(s). Game is 61 or 121 points.

Play:

The unique aspect of Russian Cross is that matches are made not by suits but by requiring the number total of connecting dominoes to add up to seven.

In the example shown, the double-5 was set. All four sides of the set double are to be played with a 2-suit so that the total is seven, $5+2=7$. No score is awarded for creating the seven combination but it is the necessary condition that must be met to play.

In the example, only a 1-suit can be played off the 6 of the 6-2 to get a seven total; a 2 off the 5 of the 5-2; and a 6-suit off of the 1 pip of the 2-1. The blank presents a special case. There is no 7-suit in the double-6 set so the three bones whose pips total seven—the 6-1, 5-2 and the 4-3—along with the double-blank are designated as **matadors**. The term matador, Spanish for "killer," does not refer to a bull fighter but to the trump card, or murder card, found in some Spanish card games such as quadrille, ombre, and solo. In Russian Cross the matador tiles are played off the blanks only. In the next game described, **Matador**, these four tiles will be true trumps, but in Russian Cross they can be played against a blank or in the

normal rules of play to add up to a seven. Let us continue with our example:

We see here that the 2-5 was played off of the double-5 set play. This may not be the most logical use of a matador since any 2 could be played, but if this is the only play available it has to be made. If a player cannot play, she must go to the boneyard until a playable domino is drawn or the boneyard is exhausted.

The 6-1 matador is played off of the North blank. The player has the choice on how the matador tile is originated or oriented, that is, which

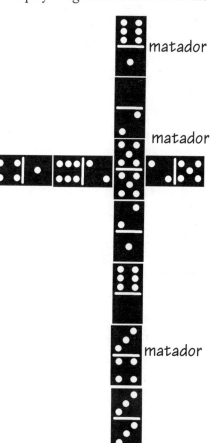

number will become the end. In this example the player could have placed the matador so that the 6 played against the blank and the 1 would become the open end. Players should choose to expose the end suit that will give them the best future opportunities. The 3-4 matador is played off of the South blank with the 4 becoming the new end. The double-3 is played off the 4—4+3=7. You will notice that doubles are played in line as opposed to across the line.

Play continues in accordance with the general rules of block games. If a player cannot play a domino that will add up to seven points she must draw from the boneyard until she draws a play or until only two tiles remain (or one tile if more than two are playing). If the player has no play, she must pass. Play continues until one player "dominoes" or play is blocked.

The basic strategy for Russian Cross is similar to all block games. Pay attention to your opponent's play. When she goes to the boneyard, notice what suits she is lacking and try to make plays which will send her back to the boneyard.

Scoring:

Scoring is the same as in previous block games. First player to domino is awarded the pip totals of her opponent(s). If game ends in a block the lightest hand wins and that player is awarded the total pip count of her opponent(s) minus her own pip count.

Loser will go first if there is another hand and will play her highest double as set play. If no double, play moves to next player in clockwise rotation. A non-blank double must be the set play.

Notes for larger sets: When playing Russian Cross with larger sets the matching-end sum-total will no longer be seven. Please refer to explanation following the description of Matador.

Matador

Players: Two, three or four players. Four players may play as teams.

Draw & Set: Two players draw seven; three or more draw five.

Set goes to highest double (excluding double-blank).

Object: To match ends that total the sum of seven. To be the
first player to domino and reach 100 points in two-player
game or 200 points in four-player game.

Play:

All dominoes, including doubles, are played end to end. Ends
are not matched by suits. Like Russian Cross, the pips of joined
ends must total seven, that is 6 to a 1, 5 to a 2, 4 to a 3. In addition
the three dominoes that total seven—the 6-1, 5-2 and 4-3—as
well as the double-blank are **matadors,** or trump tiles, and are
the only tiles that can play against a blank. *The matadors can
also be played against any tile at any time.* In addition, you
have the option of holding back your matadors. In other words, a
player has the option of going to the boneyard and drawing even if
he holds a playable domino. It is this aspect that makes Matador
unique among block games.

Why would you want to hold back and draw bones from the
boneyard? In Matador there are only two ends in play and they are
easily blocked with the blanks which can only be played on with a
matador. If you keep count of the matadors the situation can arise
in which you can force your opponents to the boneyard and
increase the pip count in their hands. For example, if you have
two matadors in your hand and two have been played, your
opponent's options are limited and you may wish to delay going
out until your opponent has drawn and increased the tiles in his

hand. When you hold a matador and decide to draw from the boneyard you are not committed to keep drawing until you get a play. At any point you can play your matador, so you can stop after one or two draws and play your matador at that time. In this situation you are playing for tempo, the timing of the game. You do not want to go out too fast and win only a small number of points. By the same token if you delay by getting more tiles you may be left holding the large pip count. In games, as in life, timing is everything.

Sample Game:

Maya's Draw:

Maya's draw is so-so. She has good variety numberwise, one matador and a low double.

Jason's Draw:

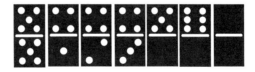

Jason's draw lacks versatility but he does have two matadors, the 4-3 and the double-blank. His double-5 will give him set. Set play is a great advantage in most block games.

The double-5 is set and requires a 2 to be played off its ends to total 7 or, of course, any matador. Maya's only response is her 2-5 which is her one matador. It is too early for her to go to the

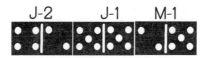

J-2   J-1   M-1

boneyard and take the chance on drawing another 2. She does not have enough information about Jason's hand to take that type of risk. She plays the 2-5, a waste of her precious matador.

Jason responds with his 2-4. It makes no difference where he plays this tile—the resulting ends will be the same.

Maya has no play off the 5 but she does have three plays off of the 4: the 6-3, double-3 and the blank-3. Since she does not have a matador it is too dangerous to go to the boneyard while she has a play—she may have to go there soon enough. The blank-3 is too risky to play because she could block herself by leaving a blank as an end. She plays the 6-3 getting rid of the higher point value.

Jason has only one play, the 1-4. Maya responds with the double-3. Jason decides not to draw and plays his double-blank matador hoping to block one end.

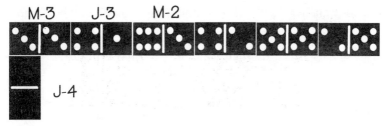

M-3   J-3   M-2

J-4

Maya has no play and must go to the boneyard where she will have to draw a 2 or a matador. There is one remaining matador in the boneyard but Maya does not know how many remain since only two of the four have been played. She draws the 5-3, 3-1 and finally the double-2 which she can play off of the 5. This leaves her holding six tiles!

Jason can now play his 5-blank. This blocks the line so that only a matador can be played, a matador that Maya does not have. She must return to the boneyard and draw until she gets a matador or until only two tiles remain.

M-4

J-5

Maya draws 6-5, 5-1, 6-2 and, at last, the 6-1. She has burdened herself with 25 additional points; she plays the 6-1. She must decide on the tile's orientation—should she leave the 6 or the 1 as the end number? Since she doe not know what two tiles Jason holds, she must orientate it for her own best play. She has nine tiles and can play off of either the 1 or 6, but her main consideration now is getting rid of as many points as possible. She leaves the 1 as the end number hoping to play one of her heavy tiles.

Unfortunately for Maya, this plays right into Jason's hand. He plays his 6-blank leaving him holding only the 4-3 matador which he can play on his next turn regardless of what Maya plays. But he knows that she cannot play because all of the matadors are accounted for. Naturally he does not tell Maya this and lets her go through the agony of drawing again from the boneyard. She draws five additional tiles, leaving two in the yard as required. No matador. Jason plays his 4-3 matador with a gleeful smile.

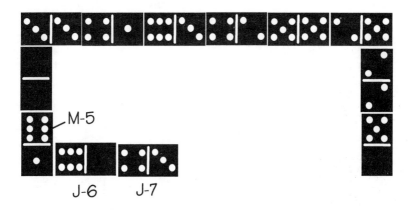

J-6   J-7

"Domino," he calls as Maya moans.

This hand was a disaster for Maya. Her pip count is 76 so Jason is awarded 76 points. This is unusally high, but it has happened to us all.

Maya will be given the chance to play set on the next hand. After the shuffle and draw Maya can play a double or a matador as set. If she has neither a double nor a matador, play will pass to Jason who will then have the same option. If he cannot play, the bones will be reshuffled, drawn again and Maya will get another chance.

Notes for larger sets: When playing Matador with larger sets the matching-end sum-total will no longer be seven. This number, which we can call the **matador number,** will always be one greater than the highest double in the set. Thus in a double-6 set, the matador number is seven. In a double-9 set that number would be ten; in double-12s, dominoes would have to total thirteen. The matador tiles would change also. In the double-9 set, for example, they would be the 9-1, 8-2, 7-3, 6-4, 5-5—the tiles which total ten—as well as the double-blank.

Blind Dominoes

Players: Two, three or four players. This game is best with three or more players who play as individuals.

Draw & Set: The dominoes are shuffled face down and players draw for set. After being reshuffled the entire deck is drawn—14 tiles for two players, 9 for three, 7 for four. When three play, the leftover tile is set.

Object: The first player to domino wins the hand and scores the points remaining in opponents' hands. In case of blocked games the lightest hand wins and scores the opponents' points minus her own.

Play:

Blind Dominoes, also known as **Blind Hughie** or **Billiton**, is a basic, simple block game where dominoes are played by matching suits. The unique aspect of this game, as the name suggests, is that the players do not know what tiles they hold and do not choose their play. Instead, after the draw, all players arrange their dominoes *face down* in a vertical row, aligning the tiles long side to long side.

The person on set turns over her first tile, that is, the bottom domino closest to her—players decide before the beginning of the game whether to play from bottom to top or top to bottom—and places it as the set play. She then continues by turning over the next tile. If she can play it (by matching suits) she does so and her turn continues. If it does not match she places it, still face down, at the end (in this case, the top) of her row. An exception arises in the case of a double. If a double does not match, it is placed *face up* at the end of the row. Play moves clockwise.

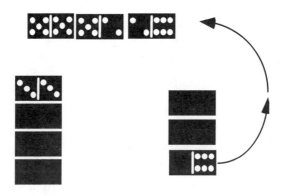

Traditionally Blind Dominoes is played with no spinners, but we prefer playing the first double as a spinner.

If a player turns over a domino which can be played on more than one end of the line—obviously more likely with the use of a spinner—he may look at the next domino in his row before determining where to place his tile.

The game proceeds in this manner until one player goes out or until the game is blocked.

Scoring:

Scoring is consistent with that of other block games. If one player "dominoes" he receives the points in the opponents' hands. If the game is blocked the person with the lightest hand is the winner.

Variations:

In addition to the use of the spinner which we recommend above, we would like to suggest one additional variation. Since the previously revealed doubles are already visible to all participants, a player may, during her regular turn and after looking at the next tile, choose to play any matching exposed double regardless of its position in the row. Blind Dominoes is a favorite with kids.

Concentration

Concentration is not technically a block game, but it is a simple and fun game, one that can be played with children, and one that will hone their memory and addition skills.

Players: Two players.

Draw & Set: Shuffle the deck face down. Each player draws one domino and player with the highest pip count will be on set. No dominoes are drawn but the entire deck is laid out in the pattern shown below.

Object: To find more pairs of dominoes whose total pip count equals 12 than your opponent.

Play:

After the dominoes of a double-6 set have been shuffled they are arranged face down in the pattern shown. The first player will turn over any two dominoes so that both players can see the pip

pattern. If the pips total 12 the player may remove those two dominoes from the board and keep them. If a player makes a match, that is, if the two dominoes total 12, his turn continues and he may turn over two more tiles. If the pip count does not total 12, the dominoes are returned face down to their same places in the tableau. The

second player may now turn over any two tiles in the same manner and may collect any two whose pip total equals 12. Play continues until all dominoes are collected.

Concentration is a game of memory, how well you can remember which tiles have been exposed and where they are located in the tableau. This is a game which children enjoy as well as adults.

Sample Game:

The first player, Dan, turns over two tiles of his choice; they turn out to be the 6-3 and the 4-1. The total pip count, $9+5=14$, does not equal 12 so Dan turns the tiles face down in their original positions and the play passes to Tricia.

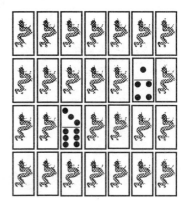

Tricia turns over two bones, the double-4 in the lower left corner and the 5-2 in the upper right corner. The pips of the two tiles do not total 12 so the dominoes are tuned face down again.

Dan has seen a match that will give him twelve points. He turns over the 5-2 in the right corner and the 4-1 kitty corner to it. Dan removes these two tiles and places them to the side.

Dan's turn continues after his last match and he turns over the double-6 and a 3-1. No match this time. Dan turns them face down and it is Tricia's turn.

Note that the double-6 can only pair with the double-blank, and the 6-5 pairs only with the 1-blank. The other tiles will have more than one match. Note also that when tiles are removed from the tableau the remaining tiles are not rearranged.

Tricia makes a match by exposing the double-4 in the lower left-hand corner and the 3-1 above for 12 points. She now turns over the 3-blank—she knows that it will match with a 9 which she has seen before, but she is one tile off and turns over the double-blank.

Dan immediately matches the double-6 and the double-blank. He next turns over the 6-3 and matches it with the 3-blank. He removes these tiles and places them on his stack. He turns over the double-5 and the 1-blank; these are turned face down since they do

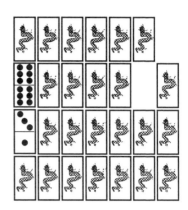

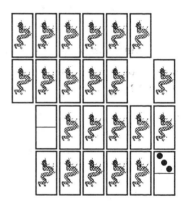

not create a match.

As the number of tiles decreases the possibilities of running the remaining tiles increases. Some players develop patterns in the way they turn over the tiles, but the only skill involved in Concentration is memory and, of course, concentration.

Tricia turns over the 4-3 and the 2-blank, still no match. She places them face down again.

Dan again remembers where the double-5 is and matches it with the 2-blank, but Dan's next two plays, the 6-1 and 5-1, do nothing but reveal two tiles for Tricia.

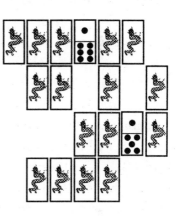

Tricia turns over the right end tile in the top row to reveal the 6-blank. She matches this with the 5-1 exposed by Dan on his last turn. She next turns over the 6-2, a tile that does not match any she has seen previously. She randomly draws another tile and lucks out by turning over the double-2 for a total of 12. The next domino Tricia exposes is the 5-blank and she remembers that two tiles have been exposed that will match with it; she turns over the 6-1 and removes two more dominoes. She next turns the left tile in the lower row and finds a 6-5, she turns over the 1-blank at the end of the row for a match. Tricia exposes the remaining tile in the bottom row and

finds the double-3. She has seen no
match for 6 pips so she randomly
turns a bone in the top row. Her
luck holds as she reveals the 4-2.
Her luck runs out, however, when
she turns over the 6-4 and the
blank-4. Only eight tiles remain for
Dan.

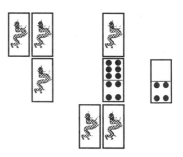

Dan turns over the left tile in the top row and exposes a
double-1. This matches the 6-4 Tricia has just revealed. He next
turns the left tile in the middle row, a 3-2, and he matches it with
the 4-3 in the top row. Dan is down to the last four tiles. He turns
the 5-3 and the 4-blank for a match. The last two tiles are the 5-4
and the 2-1 for the final pair. All tiles have been matched and the
game is over.

Scoring:

After all the dominoes have been matched the two players
count the tiles in their possession. In our sample game, Tricia had
six matches and Dan had eight, for totals of twelve and sixteen
dominoes respectively. The player with the greater number wins—
in this game it's Dan. Scoring can be done by game with the best
of three, best of five, and so on determining the winner. Or score
can be kept by accumulating points with each domino counting as
one point. A game can be the first to 50 or 61 or whatever number
the players determine before they begin.

6

Point Games

Point games are those which are scored as the game progresses. The rules of each game will explain how scoring is accomplished during play. A cribbage scoreboard is a convenient method for scoring point games but paper scorepads will work.

The general rules as explained in Chapter 3 will apply unless stated otherwise. Every effort has been made to give a complete description of the games and to cover all of the questionable situations that may arise during play, but if a situation occurs that is not covered it is up to the players to resolve the problem. As there are similarities among many of the games in this section you might see if the explanation given in one of the other games is applicable to any ambiguous circumstances you encounter.

If you come across terms that are unclear or unfamiliar check the glossary at the end of the book. All terms that are used for the first time are printed in **bold** type and should be defined at that point but we suggest that you read the glossary definition for a complete explanation.

Muggins

Players: Two, three, or four may play. Four may play individually or as partners.

Draw & Set: The players draw for set as described in the general rules. With two players each player draws seven dominoes for his hand. With three or four players, each takes five. Largest loser is setter for next hand.

Object: The object is two-fold in Muggins: 1) to score during play on end points that are multiples of five, and 2) to be the first to go out and score on the dominoes remaining in your opponent's hand.

Play:

Set play can be either a single or a double. Doubles are played across the line and play is from the side only, see *a* below. If a single is used for set, play is along the line and the ends only are used in play as in *b* below.

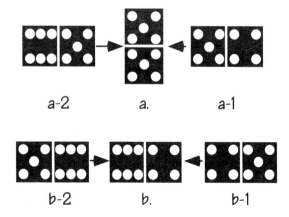

a-2   a.   a-1

b-2   b.   b-1

Points are awarded when the total of the ends is equal to five or any of its multiples. The double-5 in *a* is scored for 10 points when it is set. Similarly, the 6-4 set in *b* also scores 10 points. If we look at *a-1,* the first play after set, no points are scored. The double-5 counts as 10 since it is an end and the 4 of *a-1* is added to 10 for a total of 14, a non-multiple of five. When the 6-5 is played in *a-2* our end points become 6 and 4 which total 10, a multiple of five. This play scores 10 points.

In example *b* the first play off the set is 4-5 *(b-1)* resulting in an end total of $6+5=11$ for no score. When the 6-5 is played *(b-2)* the end count becomes 10 and those points are scored.

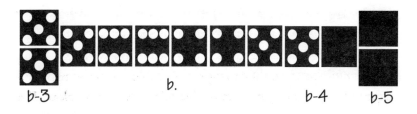

b-3   b.   b-4   b-5

Fulfilling its role as a **kicker,** the double-5 *(b-3)* is played next for an end-count of 10. This is added to the 5 on the other end *(b-1)* for a total score of 15 points. The play of the 5-blank *(b-4)* scores 10 points, the 10 of the double-5 end plus zero for the blank. The double-blank of *b-5* is played next scoring 10 points for the same double-5 end scored in the previous play. In this play the double-blank is used as a **repeater.** Blanks can often be used in this role, to "repeat" the previous score.

If a player does not have a playable domino she must draw from the boneyard until she gets one that plays. In two-handed games two dominoes must be left in the boneyard, and in three- and four-player games, one domino must remain in the boneyard. If a player has no play she must pass.

The player who plays her last domino first ends that hand; play stops and the game is **closed**. The other players or team will add up their scores and the **closing player,** or her team, is awarded 5 points for each multiple of 5 the opponents hold. When the point total does not work out to be an exact multiple of 5 you will add 5 points for the remaining 3 or 4 points and ignore 1 and 2 point values; that is, a score of 8 or 9 will be scored as 10 points, while a score of 6 or 7 is scored as 5 points. The game continues until one player reaches 61 points. We will go through a complete sample game below.

Figure 6-1 shows the standard scoreboard and how it is demarcated for Muggins with two players or two teams. The standard board shown is divided into two sections of sixty holes each grouped into twelve sections of five. A game of Muggins is played to 61 points, once around the board. See Chapter 2 for a review of the scoreboard.

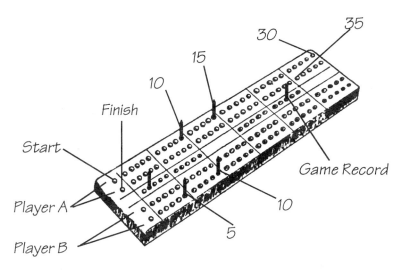

Figure 6-1. Scoreboard.

There is an alternative scoring method that is often used with Muggins and other games that score on five and its multiples. With this method instead of receiving the total point value of the end total, each score of five is reduced to one point; that is, if an end total of fifteen points is played, three points would be scored. To put it in a more mathematical form $et/5 = p$ where et is the end total and p is the points scored. The main reason that this form of scoring can be recommended is that it results in longer games, more rounds can be played, and thus skill has a chance to triumph over luck. We prefer this form of scoring, especially for team play and three- or four-player games. Try both versions and choose the one you prefer.

Sample game:

The following is a sample game between Myra and Dave. They have drawn for set and Myra will be setter. Each player draws seven tiles; Myra goes first and then Dave.

Myra's Draw:

Dave's Draw:

The first step for each player is to analyze the draw and conduct a suit inventory. As we pointed out in the last chapter, the make-up of the hand, especially the suit distribution, will determine your play options. We will analyze the available set plays, but only after the entire hand is examined can a final play be decided upon.

Myra has a strong blank-suit with three out of the seven blank tiles. She has two plays off of the double-blank; this is stronger than her one play off the double-4 or the two plays off her 6-3 or 3-4. Myra's choice for set is the double-blank. (Refer to Chapter 4 for a more thorough discussion of suit determination.)

Dave tries to keep the agony he feels from showing on his face as he is presented with a play to which he cannot respond. It is a real setback to be sent to the boneyard on your first turn, especially after a seven-tile draw. Dave's first draw is the double-5, his second the 5-2 and his third is the blank-3. Dave adds the first two tiles to his original seven and plays the blank-3. The end total is three, so Dave scores no points.

Myra plays her blank-two. The end total is five and she scores five points.

Dave looks at his overabundance of choices. He has to get rid of his high-point tiles. He starts with the 5-2. This will give him an end count of eight, no score.

Myra plays the 6-3 for an end score of eleven which scores no points.

Dave plays his double-6 for an end total of seventeen but still no score.

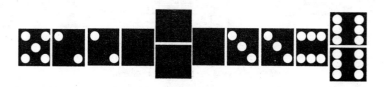

Myra plays her 6-1 for an end score of six and no points scored. **Dave** plays his 5-4 off of the 5-2 for an end score of five and finally scores five points.

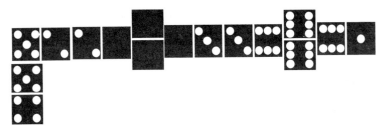

There is a traditional rule peculiar to Muggins which allows a player to take any points which are not taken by the player who scores them. For example, when Dave plays his 5-4 he scores five points. If he does not claim those points and add them to his score, Myra may call "Muggins!" and she may add them to her own score. If the omission is not noticed until after the next play, the points are lost and no one can score them.

Myra plays her double-4 for an end total of nine, $8+1=9$. Remember, there are no spinners in Muggins. That is, there is no end play off of doubles, so Myra could not play her blank-5 off the double-blank for ten points $(4+1+5)$.

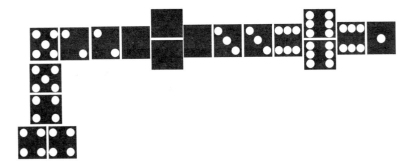

Dave plays his 1-5 for an end total of 13, no score.

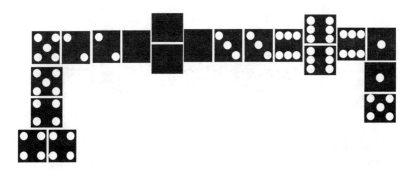

Let us now look at how the game stands:

Myra:

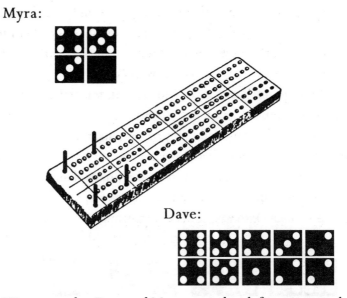

Dave:

We can see that Dave and Myra are tied with five points each, but Dave still holds five dominoes and Myra only two. Can Myra stay out of the boneyard?

Myra plays the 4-3 domino for an end total of eight and no points scored.

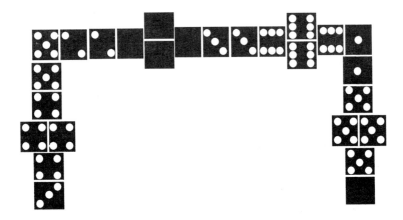

Dave plays the double-5 to get rid of as many points as possible since Myra is down to one tile.

Myra goes out by playing her last domino, the 5-blank. She scores no points for this play (3+0=3), but she will now score the points remaining in Dave's hand.

Dave's dominoes add up to 24 points, but since we score in groups of 5 Myra will add 25 points to her score. Myra ends up with 30 points and Dave has scored 5 points. Neither player has scored the required 61 points to win, so another hand will be played. Since Dave has lost this first round, he will be on set.

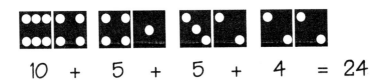

10   +   5   +   5   +   4   =   24

All Fives

Players: Two, three or four players. Four may play cutthroat or as partners.

Draw & Set: Dominoes are laid face down and shuffled. Each player draws one; highest domino is on set. Set will rotate clockwise with subsequent hands. Dominoes are reshuffled and each player draws five tiles. Any tile may be set.

Object: To be the first to domino and to score points during play. Scores are awarded when end points total five or multiples of five. The winner of the hand scores the points held by opponents when the hand ends.

Play: All Fives, like Muggins and several other games in this chapter, is a member of the **five-point family** of games—matching is done by suits, scores are made for end point totals of five or its multiples, players must go to the boneyard (or pass if the boneyard is exhausted) if they do not have play, and they must play if they can. All Fives is played substantially the same as Muggins. The main differences are that only five dominoes are drawn even with just two players and All Fives is played with the first double as a spinner while Muggins is played with no spinner.

Scoring: All Fives uses the same scoring conventions as the other five-point games. Scores are made during play for end totals of five or its multiples. Players may choose to score the entire point total or may score one point for each five. The player who "dominoes" or the player holding the fewest pips when a hand is closed scores the pips remaining in the opponents' hands. Games are played to 61, 100 or 121 points.

Bergen

Players: Two, three and four or more can play. No team play.

Draw & Set: Four or more players draw five dominoes; fewer than four draw six dominoes. Lowest double is set; if no double, lowest single is set. Lowest double is scored for two points; lowest single, no points. Play is clockwise.

Object: Scoring is accomplished by matching line ends. Any time both ends of the line match, with either two singles or the double and a single of a suit, points are scored—two points for the singles or three points for the double and single. There are no spinners in Bergen; there is only side play off doubles. There are two scoring situations in Bergen, they are:

Doubleheader:

Both ends are of the same suit.
Score 2 points.

Tripleheader:

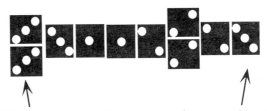

When the matching double of the end suit
is played 3 points are scored.

Play:

After the set each player in turn tries to play one domino at either end of the line of play by matching suits. If a player does not have a match, he must go to the boneyard and draw one tile only. If that tile does not match, the player has to pass. A player must play if he has a match. Two tiles must be left in the boneyard. If there are no tiles available to draw, the player passes. Play continues until one player gets rid of all his tiles or the game is blocked.

Sample Game:

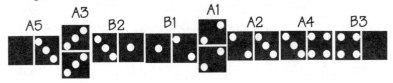

Let us look at a few plays between Albert and Betty. Albert plays set with the double-2 (A1) and scores two points. Betty plays the 2-1 (B1). Albert responds with a 2-3 (A2). Neither play results in a "match" so there is no score. Betty plays the 1-3 (B2) which results in a "doubleheader"—3s at A2 and B2—and a score of two points. Albert plays the double-3 (A3) off of B2 for a "tripleheader" and three points. Albert, of course, could play off either end and score his three points. Betty has no play and draws one tile from the boneyard. She still cannot play and must pass. Albert plays next at A4 with a 3-4 but scores no points. Betty plays a 4-blank at B3 for no points. Albert plays another domino from the 3-suit, the 3-blank, off the double-3 matching the blank at the other end for two more points.

Thus far Albert has played five dominoes and scored five points. He has only one tile remaining. Betty has four dominoes in her hand and has scored two points. The game continues until one player "goes out" or the game is blocked.

Scoring:

Bergen is played to 15 points. Each doubleheader is worth two points and each tripleheader is worth three points. Player who goes out first and calls "Domino!" scores an additional one point. Winner of hand receives one point for every domino remaining in possession of opponent(s) at the end of hand.

When a game is blocked—no player has "dominoed" and no one has a play—the hand is over. The player with the smallest number of pips in her hand scores the one point for winning the hand. While some people use elaborate rules for scoring blocked games, it is our view that the best course is to simply go on to the next hand.

Five-Up

Players: Two, three or four players. Cutthroat or team play is optional for four players.

Draw & Set: All dominoes are turned face down and shuffled. Each player draws one domino; player with the highest domino is "on set." Play rotates to the left, see Figure 3-1, after each hand. To determine partners, two highest dominoes play the two lowest. Drawn dominoes are returned to the deck which is reshuffled.

Each player draws five dominoes. The player on set draws first followed by other players in turn. The dominoes remaining become the boneyard.

Object: To score points during play by making ends total a multiple of five. End totals are scored 1 point for each 5 points of the end total; that is, an end total of 10 would be scored 2; 15 would be worth 3; and so on. First player to domino wins hand. Game is played to 61 points.

Play:

Five-Up is one of the most popular of the domino games and it owes much of this popularity to Dominic Armanino, the Johnny Appleseed of Five-Up. In his book *Dominoes: Five-up and Other Games* Armanino covers every detail of the game, including advanced strategy and the intricacies of team play. This book is highly recommended for the serious player.

Five-Up is similar to Muggins and most of the rules presented in Chapter 3 apply here as well. These sections should be reviewed if any questions arise.

The player on set plays first and can play any domino he

chooses. A 6-4 or 5-5 scores two points since they total 10, and one point can be scored if the 5-0, 4-1, or 3-2 are played since they total 5. Play continues in a clockwise manner.

Dominoes are matched by suit, with doubles played across the line. All doubles can be played as spinners. A player must play on his turn if he holds a playable domino. If he does not have a playable tile he must draw from the boneyard until he gets a play or the boneyard dominoes are exhausted in which case he must pass. In a two-player game two tiles must be left in the boneyard; with three or four players, one tile must be left. When one player goes out or all players are blocked the game is over.

Sample Game:

We will now look at a sample four-player game. After the draw, Myra and Gary will team up against Suzy and Dave. Myra is on set and seating is as shown below.

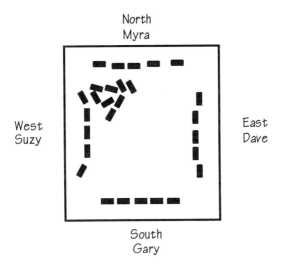

Figure 6-2. Seating arrangement for team play.

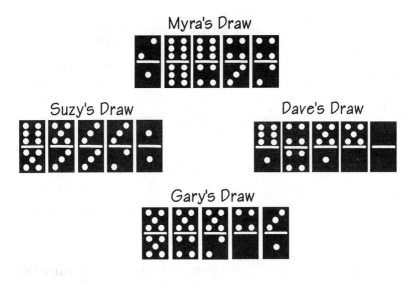

Myra sets her 6-4 and scores 2 points. Dave responds by playing his 6-1 giving him an end total of 5 for a score of 1 point. Gary plays his 4-0 for an end total of 1 but scores no points. Suzy has only one play, her 1-1, for an end total of 2 and no points. The line of play is shown at the end of the first round.

Myra makes her only play, 1-2, off the double-1; this gives an end score of 2—no points scored. Dave plays his 0-5 for an end total of 7 and no points. Gary plays his 2-5 off of Myra's 1-2 for an end total of 10 scoring 2 points. Suzy plays her 5-3 and changes the end score to 8.

At the end of the second round Myra and Gary have scored 4 points. Dave and Suzy have scored only 1 point so far.

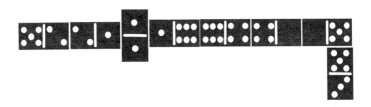

Myra plays her 4-3 for an end total of 9—no additional points scored. Dave plays 5-1 for an end total of 5 for 1 point. Gary plays his 1-3 for an end total of 7 and no points. Suzy plays her double-3 for an end total of 10 and a score of 2 points.

At the end of the third round Myra and Gary's score remains at 4 points while Dave and Suzy have tied them.

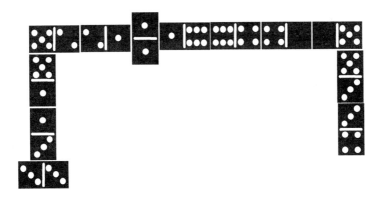

So far no one has been sent to the boneyard and Myra's luck still holds as she plays the 4-2; no points are scored off an end total of 8. Dave is not so lucky; he has no play and must draw from the boneyard. Luckily for Dave his first tile is the 3-0 and he plays it off the 3-3. This gives an end total of 2 for no points. Gary also has to go to the boneyard. His first draw is the 6-3 which can't be played. The next tile is the double-2 which can be played. Suzy plays the 2-3 off of the 2-2—no points with an end total of 3.

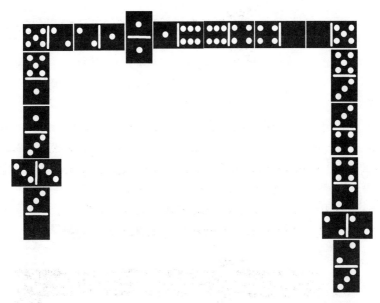

Myra has to venture into the boneyard. Her first draw is the 6-2 which she plays off the 2-2 creating a spinner. This has added a new end to count for a total of 9. Dave plays his double-blank and the end count remains unchanged but he gets rid of a tile. Gary plays his 6-3 off the 6-2 for an end total of 6. Suzy moans at this play. If he would have played off of the 2-3 she could have gone out, instead she must go to the boneyard. Her first tile is the 0-6 which she plays for an end total of 12, no points scored. Myra calls out "Domino!" and plays her 6-6 off of Suzy's last play.

Myra's end total is 18 so she scores no points, but she and Gary have won this round and will score the points left in Dave and Suzy's hands.

Dave's Hand: Suzy's Hand:

Since Myra and Gary are a team, the tiles remaining in his hand are ignored. Dave's pip total is 8 so Myra and Gary score 2 points for his hand. Suzy has a pip total of 11 so they also score 2 points off of Suzy. When the pip count doesn't work out to an even multiple of 5, remainders of 1 or 2 are disregarded. Remainders of 3 or 4 count as 1 point.

Myra adds 4 points to their previous 4 points to give a final score of 8 for her and Gary and a total of 4 points for Dave and Suzy. Set now moves to Dave for the next hand and play continues in the same manner.

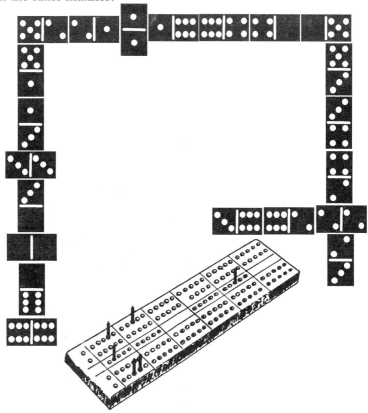

Seven Rocks

Players: Two, three or four players. Four may play cutthroat or as partners.

Draw & Set: Dominoes are laid face down and shuffled. Each player draws one; highest domino is on set. Set will rotate clockwise with subsequent hands. Dominoes are reshuffled and each player draws seven tiles. Any tile may be set.

Object: To be the first to domino and to score points during play. Scores are awarded when end points total five or multiples of five. Traditionally Seven Rocks scores are not divided by five, thus end points of $6+4=10$ would score 10 points. For this reason games are usually played to 121 or even 250 points. The winner of the hand scores the points held by opponents when the hand ends.

Play:

Seven Rocks is a member of the five-point family of games—matching is done by suits, scores are made for end point totals of five or its multiples, players must go to the boneyard (or pass if the boneyard is exhausted) if they do not have play, and they must play if they can.

The game's distinguishing characteristics can be summarized as follows. When four people play all the tiles are drawn and there is no boneyard. When fewer play, the boneyard functions as usual except there is no proscription against taking the last two bones from the yard. Only the first double played can become a spinner.

Seven Rocks is also known by such names as **Single Spinner, Texas Dominoes,** and **Decimal.**

Sniff

Players: Two, three or four players. Four players can play as teams.

Draw & Set: Dominoes are laid face down and shuffled. Each player draws one; highest domino is on set. Set will rotate clockwise with subsequent hands. Dominoes are reshuffled and each player draws seven tiles. Any tile may be set.

Object: To be the first to domino and to score points during play. Scoring is done on the basis of one point for each five points of end totals of five and multiples of five.

Play:

Sniff is a member of the five-point games family along with Muggins and Five-Up, so those games can be reviewed along with these rules. The uniqueness of Sniff lies in a special feature of the first double played which is called the **sniff**. The sniff is the only double that becomes a spinner, but unlike most spinners the ends are figured in the end score from the start.

Let us illustrate, in diagram *a* below, where the set play was the 6-4 for 10 points. The next play is the double-4 which is scored in the normal manner. The double-4 is the first double played, so it becomes the sniff. Thus, as we see in diagram *b,* the sniff ends are still included in the end count. In most games *b*

Sniff Double

End count: 4+4+6=14

a.

Sniff Double

End count: 4+4+6+1=15

b.

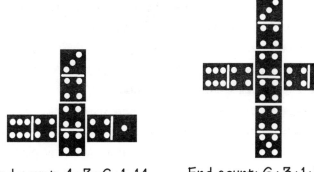

End count: 4+3+6+1=14
c.

End count: 6+3+1+5=15
d.

would be scored as 7, but in Sniff the double ends are included in the end count resulting in a scoring count of 15. When a domino is played on one end of the sniff, that new tile end is used in the end count as well as the other unplayed end of the sniff. In diagram *c* we can see the four ends that give a total of 14 points. Once both ends of the sniff have been played on, diagram *d,* the end total is counted like that of any other spinner. In the example this total is 15.

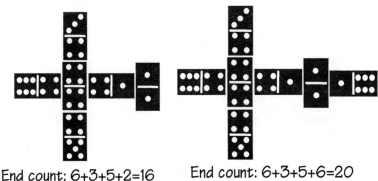

End count: 6+3+5+2=16
e.

End count: 6+3+5+6=20
f.

In Sniff only the first double, the sniff, is played as a spinner, all other doubles will be played from the sides only. They are played across the line so the total pip count is added to the end count. Once a domino is played off the non-sniff double it is ignored in future end counts, see diagrams *e* and *f.*

As in the other games in the five-point family, play continues until one player plays all dominoes in her hand or until all play is blocked. If an individual has a play, it must be made. If a player has no play, she must go to the boneyard and draw until one can be played, or until the boneyard is exhausted. Remember, with two players two dominoes must remain in the boneyard, and with three or four players one tile must be left in the yard.

Scoring:

Scoring is done as in other five-point games. In addition to the scoring on end counts during play, scoring is done in the usual manner at the end of the hand. The person who first calls "Domino" scores the points remaining in the opposing hand(s). Points are rounded off to the nearest multiple of five as described in Five-Up. In a blocked game the player with the lightest hand scores the difference between the pip-count he is holding and those in the hand(s) of his opponent(s).

Variations:

There are two variations commonly seen in Sniff. (1) Some people play that the sniff double can be played either across the line of play or along the line. Thus, in our example *a* above, after the 6-4 set the next play is the double-4 sniff. In this variation the player can set it along the line and score on the resulting end count of $6+4=10$. The sniff is still a spinner, but the "ends" do not figure in the count until tiles have been played off the sides. (2) A player is not required to play a playable domino in her hand.

Seven Go

Players: Two, three or four players. Team play is optional.

Draw & Set: The deck is placed face down and shuffled. Players draw a single tile; one with highest domino is on set. Tiles are reshuffled and each player draws seven tiles in play order.

Object: To be the first player or team to domino while scoring points during play. Games are played to 61 or 121 points.

Play:

Seven Go is another member of the five-point scoring game family with a couple of unique features. Again we will score on end totals of five and its multiples. But unlike other games in the five family, play does not alternate automatically after a domino is played. If a player's domino scores, that player may play another domino in that turn and can continue to play as long as he continues to make successive points. The player may also play another domino after playing any double. Let us illustrate these rules with a few opening plays.

Bob plays the 6-4 as set for two points. Since he has scored with that play, he gets to play again. He now plays the 6-1, resulting in an end total of 5 for one point. He next plays the double-1 for an end total of 6; he scores no points, but because he has played a double his turn continues. He now plays the 4-3 for an end total of 5—another point and another play. He plays the 1-2 for an end total of 5, again scoring and sustaining the turn. He plays the

double-3. The resulting end total of eight points does not score, but since he played a double, Bob gets yet another play. He calls out "Domino!" as he plays his last tile, the 2-4, and in one grand slam he gets two points for his end total of 10, and has gone out before any other player has had a chance to play.

There is another somewhat unique rule in Seven Go which allows play to continue after a player has gone out. If the player goes out on either a scoring play (as in our example above) or by playing a double, the next player is allowed a turn. This player can play as many moves as possible according to the general rules of the game, that is, as long as she either scores or plays a double. If the player who first "dominoes" goes out on a non-scoring, non-double play, the hand is over.

Scoring:

Scoring in Seven Go is the same as in the other five-point games. In addition to the scoring on end counts during play, scoring is done in the usual manner at the end of the hand. The person who first goes out scores the points remaining in the opposing hand(s). Points are rounded off to the nearest multiple of five as described in Five-Up.

Variations:

In a variation widely known as **Seven-Toed Pete**, the rules are substantially the same. However, the set play must be a double or a scoring domino. If the player on set does not have one of these tiles, he passes. In addition, if the player who is in the position to go out has a choice as to where to play his last domino, he must make a score if possible.

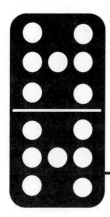

Double 7
9s & 12s

We have mentioned that domino sets come in a variety of sizes other than the standard double-6 set. The double-9 set, which is illustrated in Figure 2-5, consists of 55 dominoes in ten suits. The double-12 set consists of 91 tiles in thirteen suits. Figure 7-2 shows a complete double-12 set and how it contains both the double-9 and double-6 sets.

Most of the games in the previous chapters can be played with the larger sets with very little modification. You can increase the number of players and in some cases you may wish to increase the point objective of the game. Point games played with the double-12 can score large numbers especially in games that allow multi-spinner play.

Occasionally you will need to make a more substantive adaptation such as that required for Russian Cross or Matador. In most cases we included notes explaining the necessary adjustments in the descriptions of these games.

When adapting games to a larger set what modifications you make will depend on whether your aim is to extend the length of the game or to expand the number of players. In most cases the primary alteration will be in the number of tiles drawn. If the purpose is to lengthen the game, no modification needs to take place in the double-6 rules.

The other consideration affecting the draw is the use of the boneyard. Some games are much improved by boneyard play. In other games, such as **Trains** which follows in this chapter, the use of the boneyard is not recommended. As we have said about many decisions in dominoes play, your use of the boneyard will often be simply a matter of personal preference.

The following charts present two typical draw modifications for double-9 and double-12 sets depending on the boneyard preference.

Draw Chart
No Boneyard

Players	Pieces Drawn	
	9s	*12s*
4	13	22
5	11	18
6	9	15
7	7	13
8	6	11
9	6	10
10	5	9

Draw Chart
With Boneyard

Players	Pieces Drawn	
	9s	*12s*
4	9	13
5	8	11
6	7	10
7	7	9
8	6	9
9	6	9
10	5	9

Figure 7-1. Two typical large-set draw charts.
Individual game rules and player preference also
affect draw decisions.

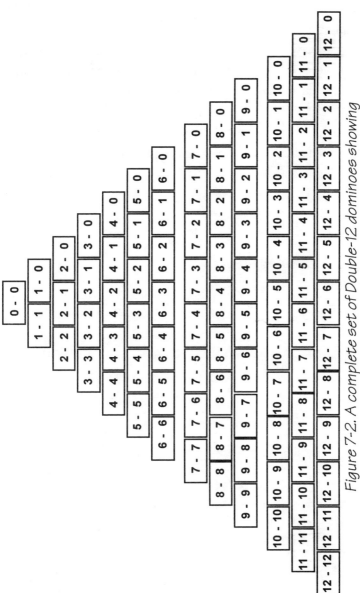

Figure 7-2. A complete set of Double-12 dominoes showing how it contains both Double-6 and Double-9 sets.

You will notice that we have not included draws for two or three players because in our opinion the only reason for that number of players going to the larger sets is to increase the length of the game. In that case, as we said above, keep the rules the same as they appear in the double-6 games.

Most of the games presented in this chapter can be played with the double-6 set, but we feel that they are best played with the larger sets. All of the games can be played with the number of players shown above.

Cyprus

Players: Any number can play. No team play.

Draw & Set: Dominoes are drawn in accordance with the *Draw Chart With Boneyard.*The high double of the set, 12-12, 9-9, or 6-6, is set play. If no player draws the high double, all dominoes are returned to the deck, reshuffled and redrawn until high double is drawn. Play moves clockwise in the standard manner.

Object: No score is made during play. First player to *domino* scores off opponents' hand. Game is 200 points.

Play:

The most unique characteristic of Cyprus is the star-shaped tableau that must be constructed before matching begins. The set play acts like a super spinner, not only can play take place off the sides and ends but also diagonally. If we look at the examples below we see that a total of nine dominoes are required to make this tableau. In Cyprus it is required to create the star before any other

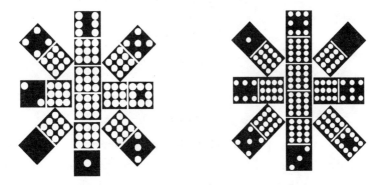

Figure 7-3 The star formation for the double-9 and double-12 set plays.

play can be made. After the set play the next eight plays must be of the high suit. If a player does not have a play he must draw one tile from the boneyard. If he still has no play he must pass and the next in order must make a star play. One domino is left in the boneyard and is not played. After the star has been formed, play continues with matching at any of the eight open ends.

Cyprus can be played with a double-6 set, but it is more appropriate to the larger sets. Naturally, when playing with the smaller set, only six plays can be made off the 6-6 set.

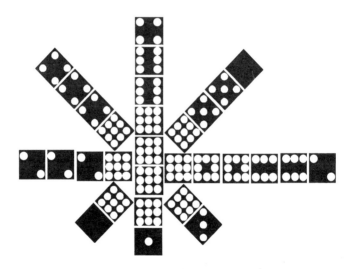

Figure 7-4. Sample play off of the double-9 star formation.

Doubles are played in line with no spinners. If a player has no matching domino then he must go to the boneyard and draw one bone. If that tile does not provide a match then he passes. Similarly, if the boneyard is depleted, a player must pass if he has no play.

Cyprus is a cutthroat game and when played with a large number of players can be quite exciting as players join together to block out other players. Alignments form and reform as play progresses. The greatest skill involved in this game, a skill that serves you well in all domino games, is the observation of your opponents' play. What end numbers are open when someone goes to the boneyard? Since a player gets only one chance at the boneyard each turn you may want to keep a player out by limiting the end numbers to those that your opponent cannot match.

After the star is formed almost every number has a play, so the basic strategy is to limit the options of your opponents. If we look at the sample tableau in Figure 7-4 we can see that after only five plays the options have been reduced from the initial eight to just five—blanks, 1s, 2s, 3s, and 4s—thus making fifteen dominoes temporarily unplayable.

As we have discussed elsewhere, keeping track of the dominoes played provides critical information. You know that each suit contains 10 tiles in a double-9 set and 13 for a double-12 set. By keeping track of the dominoes that you can see in the tableau and those in your hand, you can make a rough calculation as to what tiles are held by other players. Observation is the key to all domino strategy. Observe what is played, observe who plays what, and observe the odds of the remaining tiles.

Scoring:

The first person to play his last tile calls "Domino!" and is declared the winner. The winner scores the points held by the other players. If the game is blocked, lowest pip count wins and scores the pip counts of the opponents minus his own. If two players have the same low pip count the game is considered a draw and no points are awarded.

Trains

Players: Four to nine players with a double-9 set. Four to twelve players with a double-12 set. No team play.

Draw & Set: Draw in accordance with *Draw Chart-No Boneyard.* Highest double is set. Play is clockwise. No boneyard is in play.

Object: First player to play all of her dominoes wins and scores 5 points for every domino remaining in opponents' hands. Game is 120 points.

Play:

Each player creates her own train, her own line of play, which forms in front of the player. A train has to start with a double, the engine. Once you have an engine you may, on your turn, add cars, tiles, to your train in the standard matching manner. After you have added a car to your train—and you may add only one car to your train during any turn—you may then add a car to any or all of your opponents' trains, again no more than one car per train. If a player has no play on her own train she must pass. Doubles are played in line and there are no spinners. Dominoes may be played on both ends of the original double, the so-called engine.

Scoring:

The first player to play all of her dominoes is declared winner. Winner scores 5 points for each domino remaining in opponents' hands. Blocked games are a draw; no points are awarded.

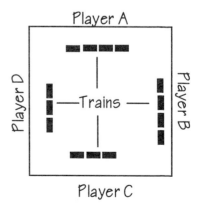

8
Solitaire

Like the playing cards to which we have sometimes compared dominoes, bones can also be used for solitaire games. The games in this section can be played with any size deck but we will use the double-6 for our examples unless otherwise stated.

All the games presented here are simple and straightforward and can easily be played by children with a little guidance from adults. Basic counting and matching skills are needed and will be enhanced with these games. Children enjoy the block-like feel of dominoes, and if they get bored with the games they can always amuse themselves by building castles or skyscrapers.

Adults should also enjoy these games. To increase the complexity or length of games you may want to use the larger sets. To modify the rules, which in most cases will only refer to the draw, subtract from the base number of the set. Thus, if the rules say to draw six dominoes from the double-6 deck and you are using a double-9 set you will draw nine dominoes and twelve if you are using a double-12 set. If the rules say draw four dominoes from the deck you would draw seven with a double-9 set and ten from a double-12 set.

Stack

Stack is a simple game of suit-matching in which you ordinarily start with a draw of four; for an easier game draw five or six.

1. Shuffle the deck face down and draw four tiles.

2. Arrange the drawn dominoes face up in front of you. You will play off of this tableau. Thus, as the game begins you have eight possible "ends" on which to play—two 5s, two 6s, two 3s, one 2 and a blank.

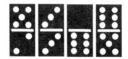

3. Draw one domino from the deck. Your object is to add it to your tableau by matching a suit on this domino with those "open" in the tableau. For example, your first draw is a 3-4. It can be played off either end of the 3-3. The next draw is a 6-4. This tile can be played off either of the two 6s or the 4. However, if you play off of the 4 you will end up with three 6s open and no 4, so the play should be off one of the 6s which will give you more

options. (This, of course, is the same strategical thought process which is used in virtually all domino games.) Next is a 3-2 and you decide to play off the open 3 of the 3-3 instead of the open 2. Your reasoning is that you have already drawn three tiles of the 3-suit and only one of the 2-suit, so you would rather leave the 2-suit open. As the gods of chance would have it, your next draw is 3-1 and there is no play.

4. When there is no play the game is over. The object, of couse, is to play all the dominoes. As was said above, you can make the game easier by increasing your original draw or more difficult by decreasing it.

Twelves

The object of Twelves is to discard from the tableau any two-domino combination that adds up to 12 points, to replace them from the deck and to discard again until all dominoes have been matched.

1. Shuffle deck face down and draw six tiles.

2. Arrange the drawn dominoes face up in front of you. Discard any two dominoes whose pip count totals 12. For example, in the draw below the 4-2 + 5-1 = 12 and can be discarded.

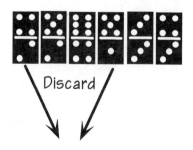

Discard

3. Replace the tiles that have been discarded with new tiles from the deck. In our example two new tiles will be drawn. The 3-2 and 5-0 replace the two discarded tiles and keep our tableau at six. We now have two combinations that add up to twelve, so we can discard four tiles.

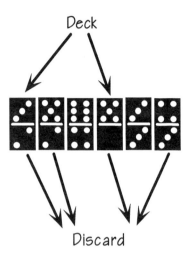

4. We must now draw four new tiles from the deck. Again any combination that adds up to 12 will be discarded.

5. This sequence continues until all the tiles have been discarded and you have won the game. If you reach the point where no two tiles will add up to 12 the game is over and you have lost.

Again, you can make the game easier by starting with a larger draw or increase the difficulty with a smaller draw.

This game can be played with larger (or smaller) sets as well, but the pip total needed for "pairing" and discarding tiles will change. To calculate this number, simply take the pip total of the largest double of the set. Thus, in the double-6 set that number is $6+6=12$. In a double-9 set the number would be $9+9=18$.

Toppling & Stacking

No domino book would be complete without at least a mention of the phenomena of domino toppling and stacking. Unfortunately we cannot offer specific tips and instructions, but certainly practice and a steady hand should be key components.

Stacking, as its name suggests, refers to the placing of a large number of dominoes on a single supporting tile. According to *The Guinness Book of Records 1995* the record for this highly developed skill is held by Ralf Laue, who successfully stacked 296 dominoes on a single supporting domino on July 11, 1993 in Leipzig, Germany.

Toppling is a true art, as anyone who has witnessed the intricate patterns and paths of thousands of falling dominoes—all started with the push on a single tile—can attest. *The Guinness Book of Records 1995* lists two categories for domino toppling. The record for the greatest number set up single-handedly and toppled is 281,581 out of 320,236 by Klaus Friedrich, 22, at Fürth, Germany in 1984. Mr. Friedrich spent 31 days, 10 hours per day, setting up the dominoes. The tiles fell within 12 minutes, 57.3 seconds.

There is also a record for groups. Thirty students at Delft, Eindhoven and Twente Technical Universities in the Netherlands set up 1,500,000 dominoes. Of these, 1,382,101 were toppled by one push on January 2, 1988.

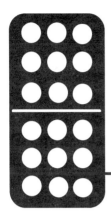

9
More Games

The list of domino games is virtually endless. With slight variations of draw, set, boneyards, spinners, and so forth, another game is born. Our chapters on block and point games cover the most common games. And the games in Chapter Seven, those for larger domino sets, comprise a couple more. Here we will briefly mention a few additional games including those sometimes called **bidding games** or, as we prefer to call them, **suit-trick games**.

In addition, we have included a brief description of the ancient Chinese game of Pai Gow. This is a domino game which is played with a set of Chinese tiles which differ significantly from the standard European set.

Finally, we present a description of Domino Cribbage. This game is closely modeled on the card game of cribbage. The domino version was popular among World War II pilots. It will be easily understood by those familiar with the card game, and it provides an interesting alternative to both cards and the usual domino games.

Eleven-Point Black Tile

Players: Three or four players; four play as individuals.

Draw & Set: Players draw for set. Reshuffle and then draw seven tiles each for the four-player game; nine for three players, leaving one tile which will be taken by the player who wins the first trick. In subsequent hands the loser of the previous hand sets.

Object: Eleven-Point Black Tile is a suit-trick game which most closely resembles the card game Hearts. There are certain tiles, called **count dominoes,** which score points for the player who ends up holding them at the end of the game. The object is to be the player with the *lowest* score.

Play:

The count dominoes are the double-blank, which is worth 4 points, and the seven tiles of the 3-suit, which count 1 point each.

There are eight suits in this game comprised of the seven normal dominoes suits, 0 through 6, plus the doubles. The doubles rank from 6-6 down to blank-blank. In the other suits, the double is the highest ranking tile followed by the **suit numbers** from 6 down to blank. Thus in the 4-suit the dominoes would rank as shown below:

As in Hearts, the object is to avoid scoring points by not taking the **tricks** which contain the count dominoes. The exception is when one player believes he can "shoot the moon"

by taking *all* the count dominoes.

Before play begins, each player studies his hand and chooses three tiles to pass to the player on his left. He may not look at his new tiles until after he has passed the dominoes from his own hand.

The player on set plays any tile and declares its suit. For example, if he plays the ▦▦ he may declare the suit to be either the 5-suit or the 2-suit. When a player leads a double, he may declare the suit to be either the suit itself or doubles. That is, if a player leads the ▦▦ he may declare either 5s or doubles as the suit. Remember, the double is the highest ranking tile of each suit. The other players must then "follow suit" if possible. Thus, if the setter declared 5s as the suit, the other players must play a domino with a 5 if they have one. If they cannot follow suit, they may play any tile. This ability to discard or "slough" is especially important in Eleven-Point Black Tile where the object is to *not* take certain dominoes. These are good occasions to get rid of scoring tiles, especially high ranking ones like the double-blank.

The **trick** is taken by the highest ranking domino of the declared suit. Thus, in our example above, the double-5 is led. If the 5-suit is declared, the setter will win the trick—the double-5 is the highest 5. If the same domino is led but doubles are the declared suit, only the double-6 can beat it. Of course, in this game you frequently do *not* want to take tricks. There are two exceptions to this generalization. One is when you think it might be safe to take the trick, especially if you are the last person to play on that trick, and you feel that you need the lead. The other is when you have decided to try to "shoot the moon," to take all the scoring dominoes.

The player who takes a trick leads for the next trick. Play continues until all dominoes have been played.

Scoring:

When all the dominoes have been played, the count dominoes taken by each player are tallied, 1 point for each tile of the 3-suit and 4 points for the double-blank. Thus there are 11 possible points. All players score the number of points they have taken unless one player successfully takes all. In this case, the player who shot the moon takes zero points and all other players take 22 each.

Games are played to 50 or 61 points.

The lead for the next hand goes to the player with the highest score. After the draw and the exchange of three dominoes, this player has the somewhat unique option of passing the lead to his left. If he chooses this option, the second player has no choice, he must accept the lead if it is passed to him.

Variations:

A derivative game called Twenty-One-Point Black Tile is played the same but the count dominoes are as follows: the double-blank counts 11 points; and the ten dominoes whose pips total 5, 6, or 7 count 1 point each, for a possible total of 21. Games are played to 121, 200 or 250 points.

11 points   *1 point each*

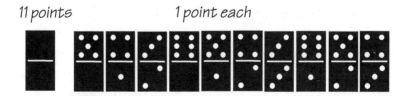

Forty-Two

Players: This is strictly a four-player partnership game. Partners may be determined by draw or by agreement.

Draw & Set: Players draw for "dealer" and then draw seven tiles each. The dealer has the last bid, an advantage, and the deal rotates clockwise each hand.

Object: Forty-Two, like Eleven-Point Black Tile, is a suit-trick game. However, Forty-Two is also a bidding game. Each **trick** counts as 1 point, for 7 points. There are an additional 35 points which come from the **honors** tiles. These are the dominoes whose pips total either five or ten. Thus, the 6-4 and 5-5 are 10-point-honors and the 5-0, 4-1, and 3-2 are worth 5 points each. These honors score points for the player who ends up holding them at the end of the game. The object is to end up with as many of these 42 points as possible and to correctly predict, by bidding, that number before the play of the hand begins.

Play:

Tiles rank the same as in Eleven-Point Black Tile—doubles rank in descending order from double-6 down to double-blank, and within each suit the double is highest, followed by the suit-numbers from 6 to 0 (blank).

In the bidding phase, each player has one opportunity to bid, beginning with the player to the left of the "dealer" who has the last bid. The first bidder may pass or bid at least 30. Any bid between 30 and 42 is allowed for an opening bid. For example, if the opening bidder believes she and her partner can take five tricks which contain 30 of the honors points, she might bid 35. After an opening bid less than 42, any succeeding bid can be of any amount up to and including 42. After a bid of 42, which indicates the belief that the player and her partner can take all the tricks, bidding continues by multiples of 42. Thus, if a player bids 42, the next possible bid is 84, followed by 126, up to a high bid of 168. If no one makes the minimum bid of 30 and all players pass, the tiles are reshuffled and the deal passes to the next player.

The high bidder (the declarer) names trumps and makes the first play. Trump can be one of the regular seven suits, doubles, or no-trump. In no-trump, the higher of the two numbers on the domino led is the trump for that particular trick. Remember, the highest ranking tile in each suit is the double of that number.

The declarer must lead a trump on the first trick. All players must then follow suit if possible. If doubles are trump, a double must be played if the player holds one. If a player does not have a trump, she may play any domino. Thus, if she thinks her partner can take the trick, she will play an honors tile if possible. If it appears the opponents will take the trick, she will try to dispose of "useless" tiles, those which are neither honors dominoes, nor trumps, nor other high-ranking tiles likely to win tricks, nor those which might be good leads back to her partner.

The highest trump takes the trick. If there are no trumps played, the highest ranking tile of the suit led wins. Remember that when a non-trump domino is led, the higher of the two numbers on the tile is the controlling suit and the double is the highest ranking domino in each suit. The winner of the trick (or her partner) places the tiles face down near her hand where they remain until the hand ends and the points are tallied. She then leads for the next trick. Play continues in this manner until all seven tricks are played. However, if either team has bid 42 or one of the higher bids and is set, the hand ends at that point.

Scoring:

There are two methods of scoring in Forty-Two. In the first, games are played to 250 points. If the bid is made, both teams score the points made—one point for each trick plus the appropriate points for any honors tiles taken. For example, Suzy and Myra bid 35. They take six of the seven tricks and all of the honors dominoes except the 4-1. Thus, they make their bid with 6 points for the tricks and 30 for the honors, a total of 36. They score 36; Dave and Gary score 6.

If the bidding team is set, if they do not make their bid, only the opposing team scores. Imagine in the situation described above that the one honors taken by Dave and Gary is the double-5. In this scenario, Myra and Suzy score 6 + 25 for a total of 31 points— not enough to make their bid of 35. In this case, when the bidding team is set, they score no points, and the opposing team scores the amount of the bid (35) plus the points scored (11) for a total of 46.

When the bid is 42 or one of its multiples, the score is the bid. Thus, if the bidding team bids 84 and makes their bid, they score 84 points. If they are set, the opposing team scores 84 points. When the bid is 42 or higher, once the opponents take a single trick, the bidding team is set. The hand stops at this point, the scores are recorded and a new hand is dealt.

When scoring by this method games are played to 250 points. If both teams reach 250 points on the last hand, the bidding team (if they make their bid) wins the game, regardless of the final score.

The alternative method of scoring is by marks. If the bid is made, the bidding team scores the appropriate number of marks. Setting the bidders scores the equivalent mark(s) for the opposing team. Games scored by marks are generally played to seven. Marks are earned as follows:

Bids 30-42	1 mark
Bid 84	2 marks
Bid 126	3 marks
Bid 168	4 marks

Variations:

Bidding: After the initial bid of 42, succeeding bids must *double* the earlier bid instead of increasing by 42. Thus the second bid would still be 84, but the third bid would have to be 168. If the fourth bidder wants to try for all the tricks, she bids 250—game—instead of doubling 168 to 336.

Play: The declarer is not required to lead trump on the first trick.

Pai Gow

Pai Gow is an ancient Chinese or Korean domino game played with the thirty-two tile Oriental set as shown in Figure 1-3. The tiles bear combinations of red and white pips. This gambling game has become better known since it was introduced into a number of Nevada casinos to attract the high-rolling Asian players.

We will not go into great detail concerning the specifics of this game which does not resemble those played with the standard sets which form the basis of this book. However, we can offer a brief description. The game is played at a table resembling a blackjack table where up to seven customers sit and a dealer stands. Each hand begins with the dealer shuffling the tiles. In casino parlance this is usually called "scrambling the deck" or "washing the cards."

The "deal" rotates around the table and all players, including the dealer, get four dominoes. From these they make two separate hands, a high hand and a low hand. Each player is attempting to form two better hands than the "bank." To win, both of a player's hands must beat the bank. Thus, if his high hand beats the bank's high hand and his low hand beats the bank's low hand, he wins. If both lose, he loses. If one wins and one loses, they tie. Each player takes a turn as the "bank." The house charges a commission on all winning bets.

Domino Cribbage

Players: Two, three or four players; four may play as teams.

Draw & Set: Players draw for set or "dealer." Reshuffle and then draw six tiles each. Set rotates clockwise.

Object: To score points according to the Scoring Table; game is played to 121 and should be scored on cribbage board. Scoring is done during play as well as at the end of the hand.

Play:

After examining his hand, each player discards two tiles, face down. These form the **crib** which will be counted at the end of the hand. The crib belongs to the dealer, so the dominoes one discards will differ greatly depending on whether one is the dealer or not.

The dealer then turns over one tile from the boneyard. This becomes the **starter.** The starter is not used during the play of the hand. It is used by all players during the **count,** and it is included with the crib when it is counted as well. If the starter is a double, the dealer scores one point which he pegs immediately. If he does not take this point, any opponent may claim it.

The first player places any tile from his hand face up in front of himself and calls out its pip value. The next player does the same, adding the value of his tile to the first and calling out the resulting sum. If any score is made (see Scoring Table on page 113) it is announced and pegged at that time. Players continue to reveal dominoes and announce sum as long as the total does not exceed 31. If a player cannot play without going over 31, he says "Go." The other person plays as many tiles as he can without exceeding 31. If a player makes exactly 31, he scores two points. If the total is under 31, and no one can play, the last to put down a tile scores one point.

Once the end of a round is scored, with either two points for reaching exactly 31 or one point for being the closest to that number, the other player begins a new round, with the rules the same as above. The players alternate until one calls "go" or is out of tiles. The last player may continue playing and scoring any points earned as long as he has remaining dominoes. The person playing the last tile of the hand scores one point.

After the tiles are played out, the second phase of the scoring takes place. Each player picks up his four-tile hand and counts all the points it contains, *in combination with the starter*. (Again, refer to Scoring Table.) The dealer's opponent counts first. This order of play can be important at the end of a close game, because the first to score the 121st point is the winner, even if the other player has not yet counted.

The dealer counts last. After counting and scoring his own hand, the dealer counts the crib, including the starter, and scores it in the same manner.

If no one has scored 121 points, the dominoes are shuffled and players draw new hands.

Scoring Table

During Play   Points Scored

Any double turned up as the starter 1

Fifteen reached exactly in play 2

Playing a tile which pairs with previous tile, for
    example, 2-4 followed by 3-3 2

Playing a third tile of the same denomination, in
    example above, adding 5-1 to 2-4 and 3-3 6

Playing a fourth after triplet above...................................... 12

Run of three or more in numerical order, although
    not necessarily in sequence order, with no "go"
    or 31 intervening. For each tile of the sequence 1

Reaching exactly 31 in play 2

Being nearest to 31 1

Counting Hand After Play

Any combination adding up to fifteen 2

Run of three or more, for each tile 1

Double run of three: three-tile sequence
    with a pair to any one of the three 8

Double run of four: four-tile
    sequence with a pair to
    any one of the four dominoes.................................... 10

Triple run: a triplet with two
    other tiles in sequence
    with it 15

Quadruple run: two pairs
    and a tile in sequence
    with both 16

Glossary

All Threes: Variation on All Fives; scores made for end point totals which are multiples of three.

Bid: An offer to make a specified number of points or to take a specified number of tricks in **bidding games**.

Bidding games: Games in which the players **bid** a score they believe they can obtain. Winning is determined by success in achieving bid score.

Blocked: When a point is reached in a game where no player has a play or a draw the game is "blocked." It comes to an end at that point and is scored.

Block games: Games where the scoring is done after the completion of the game; the primary objective is to be the first to "domino." See **point games**.

Bone: Another name for the individual domino.

Bones: A complete set of dominoes.

Boneyard: The dominoes remaining after players have drawn their hands.

Closed: Ended. When one player has played all his tiles or when the game is **blocked** and no further plays can be made, the game is closed.

Closing player: Player who goes out first and consequently scores points based on the pips remaining in the opponents' hands.

Count: In Domino Cribbage, the second phase of scoring.

Count dominoes: Tiles which score points for the player who ends up holding them at the end of certain suit-trick games, e.g., Eleven-Point Black Tile.

Crib: The tiles discarded in Domino Cribbage which are "counted" and scored by the dealer after the play of the hand.

Cribbage board: A scoreboard used in both the card game cribbage as well as in dominoes. The standard, two-player (team) board consists of two series of sixty holes divided into two rows of thirty, which are in turn divided into groups of five. Score is kept by counting and marking holes with a pair of pegs. Three- and four-track boards are also available.

Cross: Playing a double domino on a single number or a single number on a double domino; also a domino block game.

Cutthroat: Game play in which players play for their own individual advantage. Non-team play.

Deck: A complete set of dominoes.

Domino: 1) One of the playing pieces that makes up the set. See **dominoes.** 2) To be the first player to **"go out,"** to play one's last tile. The player announces this fact by exclaiming "Domino!"

Dominoes: The standard name for the **tiles, rocks** or **bones** that are the playing pieces for the family of games of the same name.

Double: The playing pieces that have the same number of **pips** on both ends.

Draw: 1) To take or be dealt a specified number of dominoes from the deck to begin a game. 2) To take one or more tiles from the **boneyard** during play. 3) Prior to beginning a new game, each player pulls one domino from the shuffled deck. The player with the highest tile becomes the **setter.**

End: See **open end.**

Face: the playing side of a **domino** that contains the **pips** that show the **suit** and **number** of the tile.

Five-point family: Any of the various games such as **Muggins, All Fives, Five-Up,** and **Seven Go,** which score points during play when the ends total a multiple of five.

Go out: To play one's last tile, to "domino." Usually results in winning the hand and scoring points from the other players' hands.

Hand: 1) Dominoes drawn by a player and those he holds at any point during the game. 2) Sequence of plays from the original draw until a hand is closed. A series of hands make up a game.

Honors: In certain suit-trick games such as Forty-Two, tiles whose pips total either five or ten.

Kicker: Dominoes of the 5-suit and the 6-1 which can be used in five-point scoring games to "kick" the score up. Note that if the 6-1 is played on a "1" it will increase the point count by five, but if it is played on a "6" it results in a decrease of the score by five.

Leadback: A tile with a **leadback number** as its open end, that is, its open end "leads back" to the original suit in a player's hand because it matches the **suit number** of one of the dominoes in that original suit.

Leadback number: Those numbers which when left as the open end of a line will match the **suit number** of single tiles of a player's original suit.

Line of play: Arrangement or layout of dominoes once play begins.

Mark: Scoring method used in certain games such as Forty-Two.

Matador: 1) A domino blocking game where ends must total a

specific number, e.g., seven in a double-6 set, to "match."
2) One of the **trump tiles** in the game of the same name.

Matador number: The number of total pips on the two halves
of the "matching" or connecting dominoes in such games as
Matador and Russian Cross.

Matching: Essence of domino play, usually refers to matching by
suits; that is, when the pip count on half of one domino is the
same as that on the half of another tile, they are said to match.
Player may add domino to **line of play** by appending matching
halves or ends.

Muggins: 1) One of the simplest of the five-point family of point
games. 2) Exclamation player makes during game of the same
name in the event opponent neglects to claim points made
during play. The missed points are awarded to the first to shout
"Muggins!"

Number: Along with the **suit**, one of the two sets of **pips** that
determine the **face** value of a domino.

Off set: If a player **on set** is forced to draw additional tiles from
the boneyard and consequently no longer holds the fewest
dominoes she is then **off set**.

On set: Refers to the person in the first position to **go out**; initially
this would be the **setter** who plays the first domino.

Open end: Any domino in the layout which may be played on.

Pass: 1) Announcement player makes when he has no further
play, including drawing from the boneyard, or when he chooses
to make no play in games where play is optional. 2) A simple
block game.

Pips: The **spots** on the face of a tile that determine the value of
a domino.

Playback: A player's ability to play additional tiles of the suit he originally played. See **leadback.**

Point count: The sum of the pips of the open ends of the layout.

Point games: Games which are scored after each domino is played.

Repeater: In point games, a domino which leaves a scoring **tableau** intact; e.g., a double or a tile which plays off a double and "repeats" the score as when a 3-6 plays off a double-3 or a 2-4 plays on a double-2.

Rocks: Another name for domino tiles.

Scoreboard: See **cribbage board.**

Set: 1) The first move of a domino hand or game. 2) All the tiles making up a complete deck of dominoes; 28 in the double-6 set, 55 in the double-9 set, etc. 3) In bidding games, the bidders' failure to make their bid.

Set play: The domino played as first move; in some games this play is dictated by the rules, e.g., the highest double; in other games the set play can be any tile.

Setter: The person who makes the first move of a domino hand; the setter is **on set.**

Shuffle: To move the deck of dominoes face down in a random manner until the deck is thoroughly mixed.

Singles: Dominoes whose two halves have different pip counts. The standard double-6 set consists of twenty-one singles and seven **doubles.**

Spinner: 1) A double domino from which not only the sides but also the ends are open to play. 2) A small raised bead in the center of a domino that helps lift the face of the domino when being shuffled.

Starter: In Domino Cribbage the tile turned over at the beginning of play which is included by all players in their final **count**. It is also included in the **crib** count.

Suit: All of the dominoes that contain a common number can be classified together and designated a suit. There are seven suits of seven dominoes available from the twenty-eight tiles that make up a double-6 set.

Suit number: Along with the **suit**, one of the two sets of **pips** that determine the **face** value of a domino. Doubles have no suit number.

Suit-trick games: Games, including **bidding games,** in which players take **tricks** by following suit, playing **trumps,** and so on.

Tableau: Layout of dominoes in play encompassing all visual information available to players; includes most notably **line of play** as well as any exposed dominoes and even such information as number of tiles remaining in boneyard and in other players' hands.

Tile: A domino.

Trick: In bidding games, the group of dominoes played and won in a single round.

Trump: Tiles which have special functions or power; e.g., the **matador tiles** in the game of that name can be played against any tile at any time; in bidding games, trumps are declared by the high bidder and dominoes of that suit can take **tricks** of all other suits regardless of their rank.

Index